ANCIENT FOREST FRIENDLY

35
trees were saved
for our forests

Preserving our environment

Indigo Books.Gifts.Life chose to use recycled paper for all print editions of this book and saved these resources[1]:

energy	water	greenhouse gases	solid waste
15 million BTUs	58,661 L	871 kg	440 kg

Printed by **Webcom Inc.**
on Legacy Book Opaque 100% post-consumer waste.

FSC
Recycled
Supporting responsible use of forest resources
Cert no. SW-COC-002358
www.fsc.org
© 1996 Forest Stewardship Council

[1]Estimates were made using the Environmental Defense Paper Calculator.

Manufacturing this book in Canada ensures compliance with strict environmental practices and eliminates the need for international freight, which is a major contributor to global air pollution

ENGLISH ESSAY

COLES NOTES STUDY GUIDE

ABOUT COLES NOTES

COLES NOTES have been an indispensible aid to students on five continents since 1948.

COLES NOTES are available for a wide range of individual literary works. Clear, concise explanations and insights are provided along with interesting interpretations and evaluations.

Proper use of COLES NOTES will allow the student to pay greater attention to lectures and spend less time taking notes. This will result in a broader understanding of the work being studied and will free the student for increased participation in discussions.

COLES NOTES are an invaluable aid for review and exam preparation as well as an invitation to explore different interpretive paths.

COLES NOTES are written by experts in their fields. It should be noted that any literary judgement expressed herein is just that - the judgement of one school of thought. Interpretations that diverge from, or totally disagree with any criticism may be equally valid.

COLES NOTES are designed to supplement the text and are not intended as a substitute for reading the text itself. Use of the NOTES will serve not only to clarify the work being studied, but should enhance the readers enjoyment of the topic.

ISBN 978-1-5526-7790-2

Coles Publishing
A division of Prospero Books
Toronto Canada
Publisher: Indigo Books and Music Inc.

Designed and Printed in Canada

Printed on Legacy Book Opaque 100%, manufactured from 100% post-consumer waste and is FSC-certified.
Manufacturing this book in Canada ensures compliance with strict environmental practices and eliminates the need for international freight shipping, a major contributor to global air pollution.
Manufactured by Webcom

Contents

CHAPTER ONE

The bare essentials

Here are the essentials for writing an essay in senior English – covering the last two years of high school, community college and the first two years of university. These eight tips will start you on your way to an A:

1. **State your thesis.** Your essay should have some point to make; it's not just a book report or a collection of random thoughts. Take a stand in your thesis statement, and then prove or demonstrate your position throughout the essay.

2. **Do the grunt work.** Major essays require research – so go to the library and find what you need. Good essays need a plan and several revised drafts before the final copy. Don't even think about trying this in one all-nighter. The process takes time.

3. **Stick to a writing schedule.** Know your deadlines and plan ahead. Use a school planner or large monthly wall calendar to chart your time.

4. **Don't rehash the plot.** Your teacher has already read the work that you're writing on and doesn't need a plot synopsis.

5. **Cite specific references and quotations.** Most paragraphs in the body of your essay will contain at least one example from your primary text – properly introduced and explained.

6. **Find a proofreader.** Ask a parent or classmate to help you spot the mistakes in logic, grammar and spelling that your computer can't catch.

7. **Get the format right.** Teachers expect a certain look for finished essays. Know what's expected and follow the guidelines.

8. **Think positively.** Your confidence will grow as you work through the research, writing, revising and polishing process. Aim high, stretch your skills and reach for an A.

CHAPTER TWO

Overview: Elements of good essay writing

This book will guide you, step by step, through the writing process, using typical senior English literature assignments. At each stage, you will get tips and suggestions for improving your essays, exam answers and independent writing assignments.

FORM: WHAT KIND OF ESSAY AM I WRITING?

Most essays assigned in senior high-school and community-college classes are of the **expository** or **argumentative** kind. These essays are meant to explain - with supporting examples and evidence - facts, ideas and opinions. Teachers use these written assignments to train students in responding, essay-style, in preparation for university and future careers in many fields.

AUDIENCE: WHAT LEVEL OF LANGUAGE SHOULD I USE?

Professional writers find it easier to begin a new assignment if they first imagine a typical reader. Knowing who you are writing for and what level of language to use makes the words flow more easily.

Imagine a particularly enlightening discussion about a recently studied novel or play among several of the best students in your English class. Aim to write an essay that reflects this level of thought and language. But don't assume that because your assignment is to be a "formal literary response" you should use language and sentence structure beyond your understanding.

Do expand your vocabulary and make use of new words on occasion, but avoid language and sentence constructions that you feel uncomfortable with. You will not impress your instructor by trying to use unfamiliar words. You *will* write effectively if you say what you mean in clear, coherent sentences and paragraphs.

STRUCTURE: HOW SHOULD AN ESSAY BE ORGANIZED?

Every expository or argumentative essay you are assigned will be arranged in three parts: **introduction**, **body** and **conclusion**. This is the "hamburger" style introduced in many elementary schools: the "top bun" is the introduction, the "meat and trimmings" are the body, the "bottom bun" is the conclusion. Knowing the purposes and usual features of each part is the first step in improving your essay-writing skills to an A level.

Introduction: The beginning of a well-written essay establishes a solid framework for your discussion. This section of the essay introduces your reader to four essential pieces of information:

- the name of the literary work and its author
- the broad subject under discussion
- the limited subject the essay will explore
- the plan or approach you will use to examine the subject

Body: The middle of the essay breaks the limited subject into subtopics. Each subtopic is usually structured and developed in the following way:

- a one-sentence opener
- a link word or phrase to connect the subtopic with the introduction
- support in the form of examples, quotations or other evidence
- a closing sentence

Conclusion: The end of the essay draws a conclusion for the reader, and includes the following features:

- a brief summing-up to review the main points in the body
- a "clincher" statement that reinforces the thesis in a forceful, memorable way

A folksy formula

An old piece of folk wisdom reduces the formula for essay structure to its simplest terms - introduction, body, conclusion.

- Tell 'em what you're gonna tell 'em.
- Tell 'em.
- Tell 'em what you told 'em.

LENGTH: HOW LONG SHOULD THE ESSAY BE?

Most teachers will suggest a minimum and maximum word length for your essay assignment. Unfortunately, many students spend too much time counting words, and then stop writing when they reach the minimum number. The results may be disastrous. The essay may end too abruptly, without completing the whole plan. Or the essay may be out of proportion - too long-winded in the opening, too squeezed in the ending.

Here's a general rule for length: "As long as it needs to be," but within the given limits. Be ready to rewrite large sections in the second, third or fourth draft stages to keep the proportions effective. Planning, even for in-class or timed essays such as tests and exams, is essential.

For out-of-class essays, overwrite by as much as one-third beyond the given word limit. Then, as you revise for clarity and conciseness, aim for the suggested word count. Specific instructions about length will vary from teacher to teacher, but the descriptions in the next section give approximate lengths for different kinds of senior English essays.

When the length is given as an exact word count, you may assume for your final version that plus or minus 10 percent is within acceptable limits. For example, an in-class assignment of 500 words should fall within the range of 450 to 550 words; a take-home essay of 1,000 words should fall within the range of 900 to 1,100 words.

Estimating your word count

Counting every word, especially for a long essay, is a waste of time. Most word processors have a word-count feature in their tools section. However, when you're not using a word-processor program, it's easy to estimate the number of words in your work.

- Find the average number of words per line. Multiply by the number of lines per page, and then by the number of pages.
- Make a note of the estimated number of words for a typical page of your written work, and use it for estimating word count on future essays.

LEVELS OF DIFFICULTY: GUIDED, ASSISTED AND INDEPENDENT ESSAYS

The length of an essay is related to the level of difficulty reflected in the given essay question. Three levels of difficulty usually apply in senior English assignments. Note that marking schemes for essay assignments differ according to the level of difficulty.

At the beginning of the senior English program, some teachers may use the **short guided essay** model for practice and review of essay skills already learned. However, you're more likely to face a **longer assisted essay** question on a test or as a short take-home assignment. Finally, by the end of the senior English program, teachers assign large projects based on the **major independent essay** model.

First review the characteristics of each type of essay given on the next page, and then check the sample questions and responses that follow. The ability to quickly identify the type of essay question and assess its level of difficulty will increase your confidence and give you more time to frame your response.

SHORT GUIDED ESSAY

- **Given information:** Broad subject, limited subject and subtopics are all provided. This type of question requires you to restate the given material as your introduction.
- **Specifications:** For an in-class test or examination question, you would be expected to produce a finished essay of about 500-700 words in 50-70 minutes. As a homework question or take-home essay assignment, you might be given one or more days to complete an assignment of about 600-800 words.
- **Evaluation:** Usually 70 percent for content, 30 percent for style. This means that the larger part of the mark is given for the information you provide, while style (including breakdown and organization) is given the smaller part.

LONGER ASSISTED ESSAY

- **Given information:** Broad subject and limited subject are provided; breakdown into subtopics may not be supplied. This type of assignment requires you to identify and arrange appropriate subtopics for development.
- **Specifications:** In class, as a test question or monitored writing assignment, 500-700 words in one class period (50-70 minutes) is usual. For an out-of-class assisted assignment, expect several days to two weeks to write and polish an essay of 700-1,000 words.
- **Evaluation:** Usually 60 percent for content, 40 percent for style. At this level, you earn more credit for your skills in identifying and arranging subtopics.

MAJOR INDEPENDENT ESSAY

- **Given information:** Broad subject only. This type of assignment requires that you narrow your focus and limit your subject, and then break down the limited subject into subtopics for development.

- **Specifications:** For an independent assignment of about 700-1,000 words you would be required to narrow the focus of a given broad subject and formulate your thesis, subject to your teacher's approval. Several days to two weeks might be given for a finished essay of 700-1,000 words.

  A major term paper is often assigned in the higher grades of senior English. You will be required to carry out research and make several choices about limiting your subject and formulating a thesis, usually with the teacher's approval. Two or more weeks for an essay of 1,200-2,000 words is a common assignment.

- **Evaluation:** Usually 50 percent for content, 50 percent for style. As the level of difficulty and length of an assignment increases, you are given still more credit for the way you organize and present your subject.

SUBJECT: NARROW THE FOCUS AND LIMIT YOUR SUBJECT

For most senior English essay assignments, the teacher will provide the broad subject, but as we've seen, the level of difficulty and the kind of assignment will determine how much you will have to do before actually writing the essay.

In this section, we'll look at typical assignments on *The Catcher in the Rye*, a novel frequently studied in senior English. Study the examples, and don't worry if you don't know the novel since background details are not necessary at this stage.

These sample assignments demonstrate what each level might require, and how you might respond.

The short guided essay: All elements supplied

Everything you need to organize your answer is given in the question. Simply restate the information in one or two sentences, then create your introduction or framework with the **broad subject**, **limited subject** and **subtopics**.

Question: *Describe three different incidents in J.D. Salinger's novel* The Catcher in the Rye *to illustrate Holden Caulfield's attitudes about people he encounters during his time in New York City.*

Broad subject: J.D. Salinger's novel *The Catcher in the Rye*
Limited subject: Holden Caulfield's attitudes about people he encounters
Subtopics: three different incidents during his time in New York City

Answer: Three different incidents in J.D. Salinger's novel *The Catcher in the Rye* illustrate Holden Caulfield's attitudes about people he encounters during his time in New York City.

Note that we've written a **topic sentence** for the whole essay to follow. This is called a **thesis statement**, and it might be followed by one or two sentences that concisely identify, without details, the three incidents in the order they will appear in the body of the essay.

The longer assisted essay: Some elements supplied

Only the **broad subject** and its **limitations** are given. Your first task is to decide how you will break down the supporting evidence. By creating subtopics and arranging them effectively, you demonstrate your thorough knowledge of what's required. You also show your understanding of the relative importance of the different pieces of supporting evidence that you have at your command.

Here's a typical senior English assignment at this level, again using *The Catcher in the Rye* as our model:

Question: *Discuss the symbolism in J. D. Salinger's novel* The Catcher in the Rye *and its importance for understanding the central character.*

Broad subject: J.D. Salinger's novel *The Catcher in the Rye*
Limited subject: importance of symbolism in understanding the central character

The specific symbols you choose will become the subtopics for your essay. In this case, it's important that you choose symbols that fulfill the requirement of the limited subject: they help us to understand the central character, Holden Caulfield. How many symbols you choose to write about will depend on time available, whether this is an in-class or take-home assignment and the marking scheme. After a few minutes reflecting or brainstorming about the whole novel, we'll choose three important symbols.

Subtopics: three prominent symbols:

1. the ducks in Central Park
2. Holden's cap
3. the carousel

Now we're ready to create a **thesis statement**. We'll mention the three symbols we plan to develop in the order we'll use through the body of the essay. In this case, chronological order - the order in time - seems to correspond with the order of their importance, saving the most important for final position.

Answer: Several symbols in J.D. Salinger's novel *The Catcher in the Rye* help the reader to understand the novel's central character, Holden Caulfield. Three prominent symbols are Holden's baseball cap, the ducks on the Central Park pond and the carousel where Holden's sister plays near the end of the story.

Comment: Note that the **thesis statement** we've created includes everything required by the broad subject and its limited version. By giving brief details about the symbols chosen, without giving away too much, you prepare your reader for what's to come.

The major independent essay: One element supplied

You are given responsibility for narrowing the focus to limit your subject and decide on its breakdown. Find out if teacher approval is expected before you go ahead. Some instructors plan in-class workshops so that students can brainstorm in groups of three or four. Students help each other in choosing a limited subject that will provide a valid analysis and commentary on the literary work being studied.

Here's our practice model again:

Question: *J.D. Salinger's novel* The Catcher in the Rye *is considered a modern classic. Justify this opinion by choosing one aspect of the novel to analyze and discuss.*

Broad subject: J.D. Salinger's novel *The Catcher in the Rye*
Possible limited subjects to consider:

- on plot: main conflict and its resolution
- on character: Holden Caulfield's attitudes about people he encounters
- on setting: New York City as Holden's "hell"
- on theme: "the unexamined life is not worth living" (self-knowledge)
- on literary devices: symbolism, satire, narrative point of view

The procedure now follows what we've already seen above, as you break the limited subject into subtopics. By yourself, or with the help of your teacher and in-class writing partner(s), you will decide what kinds of evidence you need and how best to arrange it:

- incidents to show conflict or character qualities
- symbols to help us understand characters, plot or theme
- details of setting which contribute to the story's action
- examples which demonstrate specific literary devices

An example of a fully developed thesis statement for this independent essay follows in the next section.

THESIS STATEMENT: FRAME YOUR BIG IDEA

As we've seen, in a guided essay, your big idea or thesis statement is framed or constructed for you. Simple rephrasing of the given question is all that's required.

However, for the assisted or independent assignment, you're on your own. Constructing the thesis statement is the most important pre-writing task. If carefully worded and fully understood, it will be your best guide for writing a paper that stays on track. Your task is to show that you can state and support a valid interpretation of the broad subject.

Your thesis statement is your opinion about, or attitude toward, the subject. It must be supported with convincing evidence. Senior students are usually encouraged to develop a thesis that may be challenged by someone else's opinion. State your position in such a way that an informed reader can agree or disagree with your argument. A thesis statement that is too simplistic or shallow is not the way to start an essay if you intend to earn an A.

Here's our *Catcher* model as an example for an independent assignment. Note how the introduction meets all the criteria in the box that follows:

Broad subject:	J.D. Salinger's novel *The Catcher in the Rye*
Limited subject to develop:	setting – New York City as Holden's "hell"
Introduction:	In J.D. Salinger's *The Catcher in the Rye*, the novel's central character, Holden Caulfield, experiences a kind of "hell" during his time in New York City. Three specific incidents in different settings illustrate this: Holden's hotel encounter with the prostitute, his taxicab discussion about Central Park ducks and his imaginative vision of his own disappearance in the New York streets.

Introduction: Open with a plan

- State the broad subject of your paper and the author and title of the literary work under discussion.
- Identify the limited subject by narrowing the focus.
- For an independent assignment, take a stand: state your position or point of view on the limited subject.
- Briefly identify the subtopics you intend to discuss and support with evidence.
- Clearly indicate the order in which you will present these ideas.

CONTENT AND MEANING: BUILD ARGUMENTS WITH STRONG SUPPORTING EVIDENCE

After limiting or narrowing your subject and taking a stand by constructing your thesis statement, the next step is to organize the subtopics. These subtopics, along with your supporting evidence, must be arranged effectively. If you find a more effective arrangement than the one first put on paper, your thesis statement can always be rewritten after you've developed your supporting evidence.

For a guided assignment, just follow the plan suggested by the question. For an assisted or independent assignment, take some time to jot down your supporting evidence. Simple brainstorming of ideas, by yourself or with others, is useful if you have the time.

The next step is to group and arrange your ideas and evidence. Establish two, three or four subtopics - whatever is required by the scope of your subject and the limitations of your thesis statement.

This flow chart will help you to plan. The model or template is ideal for a simple, five-paragraph essay, but may be expanded for longer assignments. In chapter 3, we'll show you how to use it for a specific model assignment. Chapter 8 demonstrates how to use an expanded version of the basic template.

TEMPLATE: THE BASIC ESSAY OUTLINE

After brainstorming ideas, begin your essay by arranging subtopics and supporting evidence using this model. An outline saves time and keeps the essay focused on the limited subject and thesis statement.

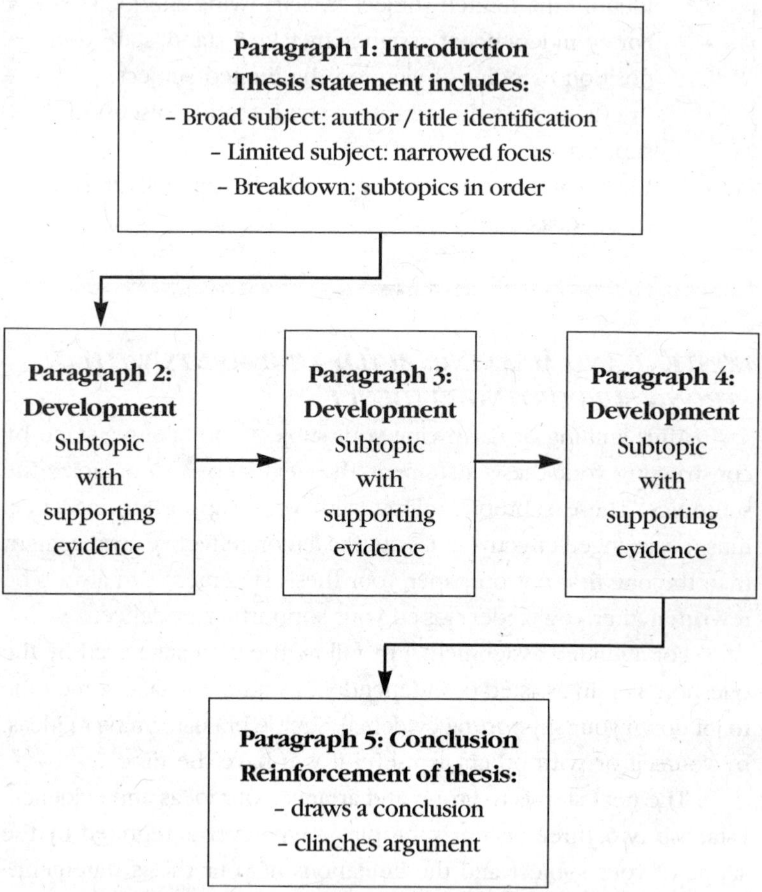

SUBTOPICS: THINK LOGICALLY

There are many possible ways of arranging your subtopics. Whatever plan you choose, the plan itself should be clear to your reader. He or she must be able to see the logical, orderly flow of ideas in your arrangement. This quality - a logical, orderly flow of ideas - is called **coherence**.

The arrangement you choose will depend on the subject of your essay. For example, a plot question will probably require chronological order, following the events in time as the conflict builds to its resolution or climax. An assignment about a story's setting may require a spatial order, describing physical details you want your reader to "see."

As assignments become more complex, the choices increase for arranging your ideas and supporting evidence. When there are only two or three subtopics, save your best idea and evidence for a climactic position close to the end.

Remember to plan - planning may be revised in the writing and editing stages. The first version of your thesis statement should be open for revision after the early drafts, particularly on take-home assignments.

CONCLUSION: END EMPHATICALLY

The ending of your essay will bring your argument to a convincing close, and leave your reader with a message that is forcefully stated and worth remembering.

Conclusion: Close with a clincher

- Sum up or review the main points presented in the subtopics. Repeat the key ideas, but use fresh wording.
- Reinforce the controlling idea - the position or opinion established in the introduction.
- Expand on the controlling idea. Suggest a broader application of the issues discussed in the subtopics.
- "Clinch" the whole essay. A relevant familiar expression or quotation will drive home your message.

STYLE: ADD FINISHING TOUCHES

Style matters. You can add a lot to an essay by learning a few simple methods for revising your writing style for best effect.

Style refers to your characteristic manner of expression, your particular "voice." Just as no two personalities are identical, no two writing styles are alike. The best style is one which uses language - diction and syntax - that is suited to the ideas expressed and to the intended readers. In a literary essay, an objective, formal style, is the goal.

Style matters

Choose an appropriate level of ***diction****: use language that is comfortable for you, your teacher and your classmates.* Avoid:

- slang, colloquialisms
- flowery language
- vague abstractions

Choose an appropriate level of ***syntax****: use sentences that vary in length and complexity.* Use:

- short sentences for emphasis
- complex sentences for closely related ideas
- link words and transitional sentences to show changes in the direction of your thoughts

Any essay assignment requires that you play three roles - researcher, writer and editor. Don't worry about style when you are researching and preparing materials, or when you are writing early drafts of your essay. Pay attention to style during the revising or editing stage of the process. Make sure all your ideas and supporting evidence are clearly and concisely stated. Keep your level of diction (word choice) and syntax (word arrangement, sentence structure) consistent throughout.

Above all, make every word and phrase count. Choose your words carefully. You won't score points with your teacher by attempting vocabulary that you think sounds impressive, if it's really language that's beyond your control.

Three levels of style

Look at the following examples, and note how the third introduction strikes the appropriate language level - it's neither too simple nor too flowery (out of control). As a model, we're using a question about Shakespeare's *Twelfth Night*:

Question: *Examine the words and actions of Viola, Shakespeare's protagonist in* Twelfth Night *and show with specific references that she receives suitable justice - reward or punishment that is appropriate for the kind of person she is.*

Under the mark: (too simple) Viola is the heroine of Shakespeare's comedy *Twelfth Night*. She is appropriately rewarded for her good qualities. She has a loving nature, patience and modesty. Her reward is winning the love of Duke Orsino and marrying him.

Over the mark: (too pompous) In Shakespeare's comedy *Twelfth Night*, Viola, the protagonist and heroine, a character with a beautifully loving psychological nature with saintly patience and the modesty befitting her youthful and virginal state, is suitably rewarded for these qualities in the resolution of the play's conflict when, after many misunderstandings and false assumptions about who loves whom, she finally and at long last wins the love and the marriageable hand of her Duke Orsino.

On the mark: (just right) Viola, the heroine of Shakespeare's comedy, *Twelfth Night*, is rewarded in an appropriate way for the attractive qualities she demonstrates through the play's action. Her loving nature, her patience through various complicated misunderstandings and her modesty as a youthful maiden receive appropriate reward in the resolution of the plot. In fact, she gets what she has wanted since Act I of the play: the love of Duke Orsino, and his marriage proposal.

MECHANICS: PROOFREAD YOUR WORK

"Mechanics" or "the mechanical accuracy" of your written work refers to your correct use of the conventions of standard English: grammar, usage, spelling and punctuation. You may work through research and early draft stages of the writing process without worrying about mechanics.

However, as you refine and polish your ideas in revising later drafts, you should become increasingly aware of the correctness of the statements you make. Proofreading is the last stage in the process.

Every professional writer has at least one editor working with him or her to help revise and correct written work. But don't expect your teacher to be your editor! In senior English courses, it's *your* responsibility to produce error-free work. Careless mistakes and inconsistencies are often the difference between an A and a B paper.

Proofreading tips

For in-class test questions or short essay assignments:

- Write on every second line.
- Leave extra wide margins.
- Make neat corrections and revisions between lines and in margins.
- Don't recopy whole paragraphs.

For take-home assignments:

- If offered, take advantage of in-class editing sessions with writing partners.
- For grammar and spelling help, join a student-tutoring program or start a study group with a few classmates.
- Use the computer's spell-check function wisely - it won't catch every mistake.
- If possible, wait a day before proofreading your final draft.
- Read the final draft aloud, listening carefully for complete sentences and accurate wording.
- Ask a friend or family member to read the final draft to you - hearing a different voice struggling with spelling and usage can be a big help.

CHAPTER THREE

Essay questions: Decoding the question words

When faced with an exam or test question that requires a response in essay form, the hardest part often seems to be figuring out what you're supposed to do. You can waste valuable time puzzling over the wording of a given question, or even misinterpret the instructions. Even with take-home assignments, just getting started is sometimes delayed by your failure to grasp exactly what is required. So in this chapter we'll look at a variety of typical senior English essay instructions, and coach you on how to "break the code" that teachers most often use.

BREAK THE QUESTION INTO SMALLER PARTS

Essay questions contain two, sometimes three, elements. The first two elements are the **command**, which tells you what to do, and the **task factor**, which tells you the object of your task. The third element, the **limiting factor** - which is not always present - tells you how to go about organizing your task.

In a guided essay assignment, your teacher will supply all three elements. The limiting factor will specify the breakdown into subtopics in detail. However, for an assisted essay, the limiting factor, if present, will be broad enough that you will have to decide on specific subtopics.

Each of the three elements - the command, task factor and limiting factor - can be seen in the following example of an assisted essay question.

Question: *Explain the causes of the baby's death, in Hugh Garner's short story "One, Two, Three Little Indians," by making reference to his mother's behavior.*

Command: explain

Task factor: the causes of the baby's death, in Hugh Garner's short story "One, Two, Three Little Indians"

Limiting factor: by making reference to his mother's behavior.

Comment: Notice that the **command word** (explain) defines the task, while the **task factor** (the causes of the baby's death) identifies on what subject the task is to be performed. This information brings the assignment into focus by specifying the object of your task. Task factors will often specify "methods," "character" or "theme." For example, you might be asked to discuss methods used to create humor, evaluate a particular character or analyze a theme.

The **limiting factor** (by making reference to his mother's behavior) further narrows the scope of your task. This factor sets limits on how you may organize your answer, but does not specify the number of incidents to use, nor does it identify which incidents to refer to. Although this information gives you a way to plan your response, it also restricts you to this one method of organization.

Avoid doing more or less than instructed. Don't, for example, waste time trying to "explain the causes of the baby's death" by referring to his father's behavior. Concentrate on several specific incidents in the story which show how the actions of the mother influence her son's death.

DECODE THE COMMAND WORD

The single most important word in any essay question is the **command**. This word defines your task and determines how you will answer the question. When these key command words appear, teachers expect to see specific types of responses in your essay. Knowing what is expected saves valuable time and reduces the risk of misinterpreting the question.

Step one, composing a simple **restatement** for any given question, regardless of your knowledge of the material, is an easily learned skill. Step two, the **extended restatement**, is based on your particular knowledge of the literary work - short story, novel, play, poem, essay - you are discussing.

Sample examination question

The explanation below for the command word "analyze" suggests how to restate the given question to begin your answer, and then how to extend that restatement based on specific knowledge of the literary work. Let's start with a definition.

Analyze: Divide the topic into main parts and comment on each part.

Question: *Analyze how love motivates four major characters to change their behavior and attitudes in William Shakespeare's comedy* Much Ado about Nothing.

Command: analyze

Task factor: four major characters in *Much Ado about Nothing*

Limiting factor: how love motivates them to change their behavior and attitudes

Restatement: In William Shakespeare's comedy *Much Ado about Nothing*, love is the factor which motivates several main characters to change their attitudes and behavior.

Extended: The audience can see these changes clearly by analyzing the behavior of Claudio, Leonato, Beatrice and Benedick in the early part of the play, and contrasting it with their words and actions in Act V to show how they change.

Comment: Some form of the key command word "analyze" appears in the thesis statement. This tells the teacher that you've understood the given question and know what is expected.

Exam preparation

Teachers typically use different command words for different grade levels, according to the level of thinking skills being tested.

- Note frequently used command words supplied by your teacher for review. Check them here as part of your test or exam preparation.
- Practice preparing essay responses by restating review questions.
- Extend each restatement to include possible subtopics. (See model for command word "analyze.")

RECOGNIZE COMMON COMMAND WORDS

Analyze **Divide** the topic into main parts and **comment** on each part.

Discuss Identify the details of a topic and consider various **points of view**.

Examine Investigate a topic by **analyzing** (see definition above) the subject matter.

Assess
Criticize
Evaluate
Judge Make a **judgement** about the degree to which an idea, statement or situation is valid. (Usually you must explain or defend your judgement.)

Argue **Defend** **Justify** **Show why** **Support**	Provide **evidence** to show why an idea or viewpoint is valid. Clearly state your opinion, and support your opinion with **specific reasons** or **examples** from the work.
Cause and effect	Identify and describe the **factors** (cause) leading to an **event** or **circumstance** (effect – that is, what occurs as a result of those factors).
Compare	Clarify a given topic by describing both **similarities** and **differences**.
Contrast	Clarify a given topic by describing **differences** only.
Define	Give the **meaning** of a word, term or concept as you are using it in your essay. Expand the definition by providing appropriate **examples**.
Describe	Give an account or an impression by using **details** and **examples**.
Explain	Clarify or interpret by supplying **reasons** or **examples**.
Illustrate	Use brief, key **quotations** or **specific references** to support a particular idea or statement.
Interpret	Clarify the meaning of a **critical comment** or a selected **passage** from the literary work you are discussing. Use solid **evidence** to support your position.
Prove	Provide **factual evidence** or **logical reasons** to show the truth of a given statement or situation.
Summarize	Reduce a literary work or concept by briefly stating the **main ideas** or **facts**.
Trace	Describe the development of a situation or event by **arranging items in meaningful sequence**, such as order of importance, chronological order or cause and effect arrangement.

CHAPTER FOUR

The process: A step-by-step writing guide

In this chapter, let's assume that you are starting work on a five-paragraph **assisted essay**. You have been assigned a broad subject, and a narrower focus for your limited subject, but you will need to break the limited subject into subtopics, and develop a thesis statement you can effectively support. Using a typical assisted essay assignment for senior English, we'll demonstrate the whole writing process, from thesis construction to conclusion.

RESEARCH STAGE: READ, REFLECT AND RECORD YOUR THOUGHTS

Most assisted essay assignments restrict your research to one primary source – the literature text studied in class. For most major independent essays you will need to consult additional sources such as critical commentaries on your chosen literary work. Methods for this additional research are explained in chapter 9 on the independent essay.

For now, in the assisted essay process, your research consists entirely of careful reading and thinking based on your primary source. Take your cue from class discussions. Class notes and handouts should help, as well as a rereading, or at least another skim-through, of the primary source.

Finding supporting evidence

- Scan your text for key passages relevant to your limited subject.
- Make brief notes on specific details, or use Post-It Notes as annotated bookmarks in the text itself.

THESIS STAGE: IDENTIFY YOUR CONTROLLING IDEA

A **thesis** is made up of one or two sentences that identify your limited subject (the aspect of the literary work you wish to explore), and your **controlling idea** (the opinion you have about this limited subject). This is followed by one or two sentences that show how you plan to break the limited subject into subtopics.

For a short essay, such as a test question or take-home assignment, create a thesis statement of one or two sentences.

- Restate the given instruction in your own words, and borrow key phrases from what is given. This core sentence will define your purpose, take a position and argue a point of view regarding the narrowed subject.
- Remember to include a reference to the title and author of the work of literature you will be discussing.
- Then extend this restatement to indicate the subtopics you will develop and support in the body of the essay.

You've now created your first draft of a **thesis statement**. Here's the formula:

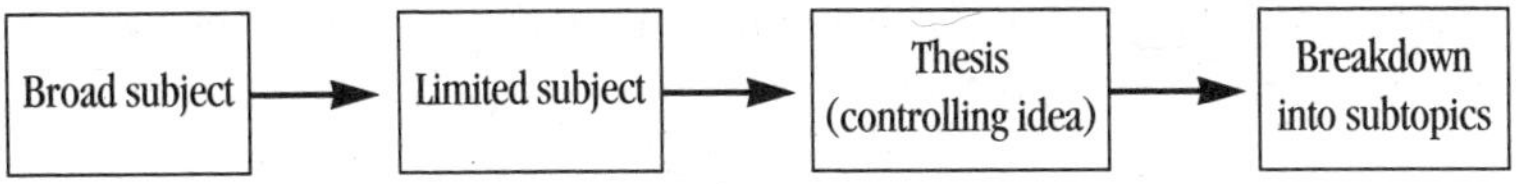

Sample Assisted Essay Question

Assume that your teacher has given you the following question or instruction for an assisted essay on Shakespeare's *Macbeth*. **Note:** You don't need to know details of the plot to follow the process for constructing a thesis as shown here.

Question: *Explain the term "nemesis" as it is used in literary criticism. By referring to specific incidents and dialogue, show to what extent this concept applies to at least three of the main characters in Shakespeare's tragedy* Macbeth.

Your thesis statement might look like this:

First draft: In Shakespeare's tragedy *Macbeth*, Macbeth, Lady Macbeth and Malcolm are three important characters who face nemesis as the play moves to its tragic conclusion. Specific incidents illustrate how this conventional literary concept of justice applies in the success or failure of each.

Commentary: Note that three main characters are named, just as the question requires. There is some indication of the meaning of the term "nemesis," but without a formal definition. References to specific incidents are not yet evident. You want your teacher to see that you have a logical plan, that the parts of your essay will "stick together" or cohere in a logical way. However, too many details in the introduction will slow down the essay and produce unnecessary repetition in the body.

Looking ahead: The logical plan must lead to a logical conclusion. Try to "visualize" your conclusion even at the early stages of organizing ideas. Plan to unite the whole essay by rephrasing the controlling idea that will run through the body. Then reinforce this controlling idea with some memorable expression, perhaps a lesson about life or a universal truth. Sometimes a brief quotation from the primary source works well, one which is relevant to the original limited subject.

The close-in/back-out formula

One good method for achieving unity in your essay is to create a conclusion that counterbalances the introduction. After closing in on details in the body, the conclusion pulls back to view the larger picture.

An effective introduction moves from the general to the specific:

- A broad subject narrows to a limited focus.
- A controlling idea breaks down into subtopics.

A forceful conclusion moves from the specific to the general:

- A review of subtopics reinforces the controlling idea.
- A broader application of the controlling idea clinches the argument.

OUTLINE STAGE: CREATE A PLAN USING A TEMPLATE

Before beginning to write, create a plan for your essay. Start by listing and then reordering your thoughts into a point-form outline. The outline form is ideal for arranging evidence or supporting materials for the arguments you present. An outline allows you to identify and preview your key material.

The diagram on the next page presents a flow chart for an assisted essay model, on the concept of nemesis in Shakespeare's *Macbeth*. It follows the simple five-paragraph template illustrated in chapter 2. The chart lists two examples from the primary source as supporting evidence for each subtopic. However, for an assisted essay of 700-1,000 words, one good example for each subtopic may be sufficient.

Draft outline: Assisted essay on Macbeth

Paragraph 1 : Introduction

Broad subject: Shakespeare's tragedy Macbeth

Limited subject: literary concept of nemesis

Thesis statement: (first draft) In Shakespeare's tragedy *Macbeth*, Macbeth, Lady Macbeth and Malcolm are three important characters who face nemesis as the play moves to its tragic conclusion. Specific incidents illustrate how this conventional literary concept of justice applies in the success or failure of each.

↓

Paragraph 2 : Development

Subtopic: Macbeth

Supporting evidence

1. Macbeth's bloody ambition and crimes (Act II, scenes 1, 2; Act III, scene 1; Act IV, scene 1)
2. Macbeth's final defiance of fate, and his death (Act V, scene 8)

↓

Paragraph 3 : Development

Subtopic: Lady Macbeth

Supporting evidence:

1. Lady Macbeth's character – evil in words and actions (Act I, scene 5; Act II, scene 2)
2. Lady Macbeth's suffering and death (Act V, scenes 1, 3, 5)

↓

Paragraph 4 : Development

Subtopic: Malcolm

Supporting evidence:

1. Malcolm's test of Macduff about royal virtues (Act IV, scene 3)
2. Malcolm's acceptance of crown, promise of just rewards for supporters (Act V, scene 9)

↓

Paragraph 5: Conclusion

Reinforcement of thesis: (first draft) Macbeth and Lady Macbeth meet with tragic ends. Nemesis for them means suitable punishment for their evil deeds. Malcolm, however, achieves the appropriate reward for his opposition to the evil that Macbeth has inflicted on Scotland. If retributive justice is indeed "just," then nemesis in its broad sense of appropriate punishment or reward has been very properly fulfilled in Shakespeare's tragedy.

DRAFTING STAGE: MOVE FROM RAW DRAFT TO ROUGH DRAFT

Write your first raw draft quickly. If you've done enough thinking and planning, and you've prepared a draft outline for a suitable development of ideas and supporting materials, there's no problem. Give yourself sufficient time and privacy to get as much as possible on paper (or computer screen) at one sitting.

Remember, for an assisted assignment, revision is not only desirable, it's necessary. Don't worry about spelling and grammar at this stage. Add new ideas to the plan as you go. Rewrite your thesis statement - in fact your whole introduction - if your raw draft has developed into something better than you'd originally planned. Rewrite your conclusion as well.

Next, it's a good idea - time permitting - to put aside your raw draft for at least a day, before returning for the first of several revisions. Professional writers know the value of a slightly different mindset after time away from a piece of writing. Your vision of the whole work-in-progress will be clearer. You'll see more readily those places where careful revision is required.

From point form to paragraph form

To turn your outline into full sentences, follow these steps:

- write your raw draft quickly
- put it aside
- revise your raw draft into a rough draft
- revise again and again: a second, third or even fourth draft may be necessary

Save an early draft

If you're working on a word-processor program, then you know how easy it is to revise, edit and correct, without saving earlier versions. However, it's important to print out early drafts.

- Your instructor may want to see the writing process on paper before you go to the final stages of editing.
- Some teachers base part of the final mark on evidence you present of the actual writing process, including rough drafts you've edited.
- A paper version is easier to share with another reader during revision stages.
- Sometimes you'll want to use a phrase from draft two in draft five, long after the file has been erased.

Taking each rough draft to the next version may require extensive rewriting. The most important part of this stage is improving the flow of ideas while keeping your coherent and logical organization obvious. Be flexible. If possible, share your work with someone whose writing skills you trust - a friend, family member or classmate. Make use of those suggestions you feel will strengthen the essay.

Backup files

Save each draft under a new file name - "Macbeth 1," "Macbeth 2," etc. - on a separate floppy disk. Then you'll always have a backup if the hard drive crashes.

Supporting Evidence: Select your key passages

For most assisted essays, use the primary source, your textbook, for evidence to support ideas in the body of the essay. The key passages already noted in your preliminary research will provide this evidence. These passages may include descriptions of settings, or incidents relating to character development - whatever you need to support your controlling idea. Make note of these key passages on your draft outline.

As you write and revise your rough drafts, keep these suggestions in mind. First, use quotations sparingly. It's often better to paraphrase - restate in your own words - to show that you fully understand the material you are presenting. Second, keep each selected quotation short - one or two lines of print - and fit it into the grammar of your own sentence.

Follow two rules when you paraphrase or quote. First, use double quotation marks around all words taken directly from your source. Second, use parentheses to note the exact source after each quotation or paraphrased passage as follows:

- For a story, novel or modern play, give page reference in parentheses: (47).
- For a poem, give line reference in parentheses: (l. 16) or (ll. 16-23).
- For a Shakespearean play, give act, scene and line reference in parentheses: (III.2.27).

REVISION STAGE: FOCUS ON YOUR THESIS

Rethink and revise each part of the essay, until you are satisfied that you have the clearest version of your thesis, and the most logical arrangement for subtopics and supporting evidence. During revision, refer regularly to your introduction. Revise the introduction if necessary, but don't lose sight of what was originally required for the assignment.

Do a quick inventory of what you've accomplished so far using the checklist below. Try to analyze the substance of the whole essay as if it were someone else's work. Look for weak spots. You want to strengthen the logical flow of ideas (**coherence**), focus on one subject and its related subtopics (**unity**), and stress your important ideas (**emphasis**). That's the **CUE** to good writing.

Substance: Revision checklist

Introduction

- ❑ Is the thesis clearly worded?
- ❑ Is a logical plan introduced and then followed in the body of the essay?

Body

- ❑ Are links - words, phrases, short sentences - used between paragraphs of the essay?
- ❑ Are strong ideas emphasized in the subtopics?
- ❑ Is supporting evidence adequate and convincing?
- ❑ Has off-topic material been eliminated?

Conclusion

- ❑ Is the thesis reinforced in the conclusion?
- ❑ Is there a clincher at the end - a catchy phrase or short quotation relevant to the limited subject and controlling idea?

CHAPTER FIVE

Substance: Make a good essay better

The next step of the essay process is the polishing stage, to produce your second-last draft before your final "fair copy." This polishing stage consists of three steps - strengthening substance, improving style and perfecting mechanics.

First, let's work on substance. We'll build better arguments from thesis to conclusion by refining and clarifying everything we've written so far.

REFINE YOUR THESIS

Sometimes during the writing and revising process, the subject takes on a life of its own. Arguments may develop into areas not entirely expected by you or covered by your original thesis statement, even though you're still on topic. It's important to be flexible. Your thesis statement is not carved in stone. Revise it as needed, right up to the final draft - but within the limits of the specific subject and your teacher's instructions.

Refining the thesis – How it's done

Step 1: Make the logic clear in your arrangement of subtopics.

Step 2: Move from the general to the specific by using words that are precise and accurate.

Step 3: State or suggest the reason for developing the subtopics: why is the subject relevant or important?

We'll go back to the example we worked on in chapter 4: the concept of nemesis in Shakespeare's *Macbeth*. Here are the instructions for this assisted essay:

Question: *Explain the term "nemesis" as it is used in literary criticism. By referring to specific incidents and dialogue, show to what extent this concept applies to at least three of the main characters in Shakespeare's tragedy* Macbeth.

In the next section, compare each draft version of the thesis with the corresponding commentary that follows.

Model thesis statement: Nemesis in Macbeth

(see outline in chapter 4)

First draft: In Shakespeare's tragedy *Macbeth*, Macbeth, Lady Macbeth and Malcolm are three important characters who face nemesis as the play moves to its tragic conclusion. Specific incidents illustrate how this conventional literary concept of justice applies in the success or failure of each.

Second draft: In Shakespeare's Scottish tragedy, Lady Macbeth, Macbeth and Malcolm are three important characters for whom nemesis means punishment or reward. As the play moves to a conclusion that brings tragedy for Macbeth and a promising future for Scotland, specific incidents in the order they occur illustrate how this conventional literary concept of justice applies.

Polished thesis: Nemesis, as a literary concept, means appropriate vengeance and punishment for evil actions, but extends to include appropriate reward for good actions. As Shakespeare's *Macbeth* swiftly moves to a conclusion that brings tragedy for Macbeth and a promising future for Scotland, specific incidents in chronological order illustrate nemesis as just retribution: punishment first for Lady Macbeth, then for Macbeth; and finally, reward for Malcolm.

Commentary

First draft: This is satisfactory as a thesis statement, since it is an accurate restatement of the given question. An adequate framework provides for the development of three subtopics - three important characters listed without elaboration. However, there are weaknesses:

- If there is logic in the plan for the order of the subtopics, that logic is not clear.
- No attempt is made to extend the thesis further by explaining the concept of nemesis or suggesting how it applies.
- Wording is awkward: title character immediately follows the play title.

Second draft: Note these features of our revised thesis:

- The order of subtopics now seems to have a logical plan, although it is still not clearly stated: in chronological order, Lady Macbeth is first victim, Macbeth is second, and Malcolm is third.
- A preliminary attempt is made to explain that the concept of nemesis as used in this essay includes both punishment and reward.
- The awkward wording of the title reference in the first draft is avoided.

Polished thesis: This **extended** thesis statement exceeds the expectations implied in the given instructions. Additional substance and insight is added in these features:

- A broad definition of nemesis is developed.
- Two opposing kinds of just retribution are appropriately linked to the characters chosen as subtopics.
- The plan is obvious: the order of subtopics is clearly chronological, according to when each of the three characters comes to a tragic or fortunate end.

TIGHTEN YOUR LINKS

Linking the paragraphs in the body of your essay is important for achieving coherence. The reader must see and follow a logical plan through the essay from introduction to conclusion.

Tightening links – How it's done

Method 1: Use the word "first" near the start of your first subtopic. Each of the following subtopics would begin with "second" or "third" or "fourth" - as many as are needed.

Method 2: Repeat a key word or phrase from the thesis statement at or near the start of each subtopic

The following two examples of linking devices illustrate a basic and an advanced method for achieving coherence. We'll work from the polished version of our thesis.

Polished thesis: Nemesis, as a literary concept, means appropriate vengeance and punishment for evil actions, but extends to include appropriate reward for good actions. As Shakespeare's *Macbeth* swiftly moves to a conclusion that brings tragedy for Macbeth and a promising future for Scotland, specific incidents in chronological order illustrate nemesis as just retribution: punishment first for Lady Macbeth, then for Macbeth; and finally, reward for Malcolm.

Linking method 1: The *first* major character to be given suitable punishment is Lady Macbeth, whose vicious words and deeds in the early part of the play lead to madness and death.

Linking method 2: After her vicious words and deeds in the early part of the play, *nemesis* - appropriate punishment - comes to Lady Macbeth in the form of madness and death.

Commentary

Linking method 1 – Numerical:

This method is efficient in a short essay, especially when time is a factor on an in-class exam or assignment. The reader recognizes immediately each stage of the logical arrangement.

Linking method 2 – Repetition:

This is a more subtle method, suitable for longer take-home assignments, and also provides an effective coherence-link for the reader. In our example, the word "nemesis" and the phrase "appropriate punishment," or some variation of that phrase, will provide the link for each subtopic.

CLARIFY AND EXPAND YOUR SUBTOPICS

The information to build your arguments must be stated simply and directly. However, you must be considerate to the reader – expand the information and guide your teacher step by step through the arguments. Define your terms. Explain how your evidence supports each subtopic. Convince the teacher that your presentation of evidence is thorough and accurate.

Expanding a subtopic – How it's done

Step 1: Use key words from the essay thesis statement to create a "mini-thesis" for each subtopic. This serves to link your subtopic to the controlling idea in the introduction.

Step 2: Identify and define specific terms relevant to each subtopic.

Step 3: Select and arrange the *best* examples and other supporting evidence.

Step 4: Clinch the argument with a strong concluding statement.

In the polished third draft of our thesis statement on nemesis in Shakespeare's *Macbeth*, we've not only defined the key word for this essay, we've also stated how the expanded definition will apply to each of the three characters chosen as subtopics.

Polished thesis: Nemesis, as a literary concept, means appropriate vengeance and punishment for evil actions, but extends to include appropriate reward for good actions. As Shakespeare's *Macbeth* swiftly moves to a conclusion that brings tragedy for Macbeth and a promising future for Scotland, specific incidents in chronological order illustrate nemesis as just retribution: punishment first for Lady Macbeth, then for Macbeth; and finally, reward for Malcolm.

We'll choose the first subtopic about Lady Macbeth to demonstrate how to expand the information, developing and strengthening the argument.

Smooth moves

Choose linking words and phrases for smooth transitions between paragraphs, or between sentences within a paragraph. Here are six of the most common links:

however	for example
therefore	in addition
finally	on the other hand

Model first subtopic: Nemesis for Lady Macbeth

❶ After her vicious words and deeds in the early part of the play, *nemesis* – appropriate punishment – comes to Lady Macbeth in the form of madness and death. ❷ In the first act, as soon as she reads Macbeth's letter about his meeting the Weird Sisters, Lady Macbeth's ambitions on his behalf (and her own) are clear. ❸ Nothing, she says, must prevent them from achieving "the golden round," the crown of Scotland (I.5.28), and she invokes evil spirits to fill her "top-full / Of direst cruelty" (I.5.42). ❹ Her thoughts are bloodthirsty, and during the scene of the murder of King Duncan, her hands are bloody. ❺ She smears them with Duncan's blood when she returns to the scene of the crime to implicate the guards. ❻ Shakespeare plants the idea of nemesis at this early stage, when Lady Macbeth calmly suggests, "A little water clears us of this deed" (II.2.66). ❼ This will not be possible. ❽ The evil within her character finds an outlet in the last act. ❾ Ironically, in her mad sleepwalking, Lady Macbeth finds it impossible to wash the imagined blood from her guilty hands. ❿ She cries, "Out damned spot!" and goes on to ask, "What, will these hands ne'er be clean?" (V.1.33, 41). ⓫ Her own conscience has become the agent of nemesis demanding vengeance for her crimes, but "a little water" cannot cleanse a nature so stained by evil. ⓬ Although the sleepwalking scene evokes pity in the audience, we cannot help feeling satisfied that justice has been appropriately served when Macbeth hears the report of her death (V.5.16). ⓭ In the classical tradition of Greek tragedy, the goddess Nemesis was the instrument of the gods' vengeance for unspeakable human crimes. ⓮ In the punishment of Lady Macbeth, her madness and death, Shakespeare has used the concept of nemesis in exactly the same way.

Commentary

Opening: The mini-thesis (sentence ❶) for the first subtopic in our model uses the second coherence-link method: the repetition of key words from the essay thesis, "nemesis" and "appropriate punishment."

Coherence: To develop this subtopic, the writer identifies the evil in Lady Macbeth's character and deeds that will deserve punishment (❷-❺).

Supporting evidence: Notes in the school edition of the play (primary source), and the student's preliminary research notes provide appropriate brief quotations and references to specific incidents. These illustrate the evil in Lady Macbeth and the punishment she receives. (❻-⓬)

Closing: The closing sentences (⓭-⓮) summarize this subtopic, and generalize with a brief reference to the traditional concept of nemesis. The student unifies this paragraph, and links it very competently to the thesis statement. Repeated key words and phrases as links include "vengeance," "crimes," "punishment" and "nemesis."

USE YOUR SUPPORTING EVIDENCE EFFECTIVELY

Presenting the supporting evidence in an effective way can often make the difference between a B and an A essay. Too many students simply drop in their supporting evidence, leaving the teacher to figure out how and why it is relevant and important.

The following three examples demonstrate how a quotation from *Macbeth* might be used to illustrate nemesis for Lady Macbeth. In each case, a short quotation (less than two lines) is integrated into the essay-writer's sentence.

Using evidence effectively – How it's done

Step 1: Introduce your evidence with a brief explanation about why you are using it. This applies to quoting, paraphrasing or summarizing.

Step 2: If quoting, quote accurately, but be concise as well. Don't quote 10 lines of dialogue or a whole paragraph if you can make your point with one sentence or a short phrase.

Step 3: Follow a longer piece of evidence with a brief summary comment to confirm your reason for using it.

First draft: (inadequate) Punishment for the evil within Lady Macbeth first takes the form of madness. She tries to wash imaginary blood from her hands, crying, "Out damned spot! . . . What, will these hands ne'er be clean?" (V.1.33, 41)

Second draft: (satisfactory) Punishment for the evil within Lady Macbeth first takes the form of madness. In Act V, she appears demented, walking in her sleep and trying to wash imaginary blood from her hands. Anxiously she cries, "Out damned spot! . . . What, will these hands ne'er be clean?" (V.1.33, 41)

Third draft: (superior)

The evil within her character finds an outlet in the last act. Ironically, in her mad sleepwalking, Lady Macbeth finds it impossible to wash the imagined blood from her guilty hands. She cries, "Out damned spot!" and goes on to ask, "What, will these hands ne'er be clean?" (V.1.33, 41). Her own conscience has become the agent of nemesis demanding vengeance for her crimes, but "a little water" cannot cleanse a nature so stained by evil.

(**Note**: this third draft appears as sentences 8–11 in the model used previously.)

Commentary

First draft: The writer does not clearly sketch in the situation, and does not show that Lady Macbeth's actions constitute madness or deserved punishment.

Second draft: An indication of the context helps us in visualizing the scene, but there is still only a brief explanation as to how madness is a feature of nemesis punishing Lady Macbeth.

Third draft: The scene is sketched in and the quotations used as supporting evidence are fully explained. The role of nemesis is stressed, as appropriate and ironic punishment (relating this scene to Lady Macbeth's earlier statement "A little water clears us of this deed").

STRENGTHEN YOUR CONCLUSION

You know from chapters 2 and 4 the elements of a good conclusion. Its primary purpose is to bring your argument to a forceful close (emphasis). However, strong conclusions have two additional purposes: to complete the logical plan (coherence), and to unify the whole essay (unity). Together, these three support the **CUE** to good writing:

- **Coherence:** A strong conclusion completes the logical plan of the whole essay. It demonstrates that the thesis statement and the breakdown into subtopics have been presented and supported.
- **Unity:** A strong conclusion unifies the whole essay by linking the conclusion to the introduction.
- **Emphasis:** A strong conclusion leaves the reader with a memorable impression.

Concluding forcefully – How it's done

Step 1: Use key words from the essay introduction one last time.

Step 2: Find the common thread that runs through the subtopics. Remind the reader of the evidence selected and explained throughout the essay.

Step 3: Suggest an appropriate universal truth by citing a familiar proverb or a relevant quotation from the primary source.

***Model conclusion: Nemesis in* Macbeth**

Here's how we might finish off our essay on the concept of nemesis as it applies to three important characters in Shakespeare's *Macbeth*. We'll start again from our draft outline in chapter 4.

First draft: (adequate) Macbeth and Lady Macbeth meet with tragic ends. Nemesis for them means suitable punishment for their evil deeds. Malcolm, however, achieves the appropriate reward for his opposition to the evil that Macbeth has inflicted on Scotland. If retributive justice is indeed "just," then nemesis in its broad sense of appropriate punishment or reward has been very properly fulfilled in Shakespeare's tragedy.

Second draft: (superior) ❶ The deaths of Lady Macbeth and Macbeth are indeed tragic, for both characters evoke sympathy and even admiration in the early part of the play. ❷ However, when their inherent evil takes them too far, nemesis catches up with them, and they suffer appropriate punishment – death for their crimes. ❸ But nemesis in its broad sense includes reward for good actions as well. ❹ Malcolm finally inherits his father's crown, his reward for opposing the evil brought upon his suffering country by Macbeth. ❺ Retributive justice, as developed in this play, is indeed "just." ❻ Malcolm's final promise, to his country and his countrymen, suggests that nemesis has played its part, and that God's Grace will now return to Scotland:

What needful else
That calls upon us, by the grace of Grace,
We will perform in measure, time, and place.
(V.9.37–39)

Commentary

First draft: The opening sentence contains a much simplified reference to the "tragedy" mentioned in our polished introduction. The phrase "suitable punishment" needs to be more precisely defined and summarized here. References to the evidence presented in the essay are limited to the phrase "retributive justice is indeed 'just.'" We need more elaboration. The essay's controlling idea - that nemesis is complete, and Scotland's promising future is in good hands - needs reinforcement.

Second draft: Sentences ❶ - ❷ summarize the subtopics and identify the common thread, by reviewing the punishment and reward handed out as nemesis. The controlling idea - retributive justice that is indeed "just" - is also reinforced by the special emphasis on Malcolm's promise to his countrymen about Scotland's future (sentences ❺ - ❻). This idea is appropriately supported with a quotation from his last speech in the play, where the concept of God's Grace replaces the old ideas of crime, vengeance and punishment.

Thus **coherence** is sustained by reminding the reader of the supporting evidence used in the essay, incidents of punishment and reward. **Unity** is maintained by repeating key words and ideas, such as "nemesis," "appropriate," "punishment," "reward" and "promising" from the introduction. Finally, **emphasis** is achieved by using a clincher statement, a generalizing comment about Scotland's future, supported by a quotation from the new king's final words in the play.

CHAPTER SIX

Style: Fine-tune the details

In chapters 2 to 5, we illustrated how to limit a general subject, formulate a thesis statement and move from the "raw" draft through several revisions. Now we'll look at more specific techniques for moving a competent essay from a B to an A in your instructor's mark book.

Defining your style

Your clothing defines your personal image. But you do adopt different styles of dress depending on the occasion - jeans and sneakers for a movie with friends, a cap and gown for graduation ceremonies. Your choice of clothing creates a characteristic style suitable to the occasion.

In the same way, your choice of words (diction) and how you use them in varied sentence structures and paragraph organization (syntax) define your writing style. When your teacher assigns a personal, creative response, wear your jeans and sneakers. For a formal, literary essay, put on your cap and gown. In this chapter, we'll show you seven tips to ensure your writing style meets the formal essay requirements of your teacher.

The following examples are drawn from senior English essays.

SEVEN TIPS FOR SELECTING THE RIGHT WORDS

TIP 1: Choose words carefully.

Rule: Choose words that explain ideas and arguments clearly. Rephrase imprecise wording to accurately express your meaning.

Example: Shakespeare's *Hamlet*

(b) **Original:** Hamlet's words and actions show that he is crazy.

(b) **Revised:** Hamlet's words and actions show that he may lose his rational restraints in emotional outbursts close to hysteria, but he never completely loses control as does a victim of true madness.

Explanation: In sentence (a), the word "crazy" is too general and vague as a comment or opinion to be useful. The revised sentence (b) explains more clearly the problem of judging Hamlet's words and actions. Whether you agree with this revised statement or not, it provides a real basis for further comment and debate.

TIP 2: Use vivid verbs.

Rule: Use vigorous verbs that express action. Give your writing more energy by replacing verbs that merely connect ideas. The most important word in any sentence is usually the verb.

Example: Shakespeare's *Othello*

(a) **Original:** Othello is a military leader who is capable of decisive actions and quick solutions to problems.

(b) **Revised:** As a military leader, Othello acts decisively and solves problems quickly.

Explanation: Sentence (b) states the idea more directly and more succinctly. Writing is clearer and more emphatic when you choose verbs that in themselves are "loaded" - they have power to inform and convince.

TIP 3: Chop deadwood.

Rule: Eliminate deadwood - repetitive, unnecessary wording that obscures meaning.

Example: Shakespeare's *Much Ado about Nothing*

(a) **Original:** Claudio learns the truth and grasps what has happened only after Don John's villainous plot is revealed and his evil deeds exposed.

(b) **Revised:** Claudio grasps what has happened when Don John's evil plot is exposed.

Explanation: Sentence (b) is clearer, more concise, more emphatic.

Don't get personal

Although we're using an informal style in this book, don't do the same in your essays. Keep these suggestions in mind:

- Maintain a level of formality by avoiding the first and second-person pronouns: "I," "me," "we," "us," and "you."
- Steer clear of contractions such as "isn't" and "don't."
- Use an impersonal or objective style to refer to "the reader," or "the audience," whichever is appropriate to the work studied.

TIP 4: Avoid clichés, jargon and mixed metaphors.

Rule: Eliminate expressions that are too familiar (clichés), too specialized in meaning (jargon) or too confusing because they mix two or more images (mixed metaphors). The simplest, most direct way of expressing an idea is usually the best.

Example: J.D. Salinger's *The Catcher in the Rye*

(a) **Original:** Holden Caulfield, the protagonist, is a sadder but wiser person at the end of his experiences in New York City. He is paranoid about other people, and is unwilling to place bets on a rose-colored future.

(b) **Revised:** By the end of his experiences in New York City, Holden Caulfield, the protagonist, is suffering, but has learned a great deal. He no longer trusts other people, and he is unsure about his future.

Explanation: In sentence (a), the cliché "sadder but wiser" lacks freshness and therefore has no impact on the reader. In fact, clichés such as "sadder but wiser" often de-emphasize ideas, because we pay little attention to them. The word "paranoid," common in everyday speech (and usually incorrect) is medical jargon. Its precise medical meaning may or may nor apply to Holden, but the writer of this sentence should clarify the intended meaning here. The end of the sentence is entertaining, but it's an unclear mix of metaphors, one from gambling and the other from the old cliché about "looking through rose-colored spectacles."

TIP 5: Reword awkward spots.

Rule: Revise indirect and awkward phrasing.

Example: W.O. Mitchell's *Who Has Seen the Wind*

(a) **Original:** It is through indirect suggestions to the reader that the narrator, in the novel's conclusion, shows that his young central character, Brian, is on his first steps to maturity. His past can be nostalgically appreciated, and at the same time, his future can be anticipated.

(b) **Revised:** By indirect suggestions, the narrator, in the novel's conclusion, shows that his young protagonist, Brian, is growing up. Brian can nostalgically appreciate the past, and at the same time look forward to his future.

Explanation: The revised passage (b) is clearer and more concise. The writer avoids the indirect and awkward wording at the start ("It is in . . . . "), and changes the passive constructions ("can be . . . appreciated," "can be anticipated") into active forms.

Awkward wording fails to express meanings clearly because faulty diction or poor syntax may confuse the reader. Replacing a single word or phrase sometimes helps, but often whole sentences must be reconstructed.

TIP 6: Avoid pompous wording and "purple" prose.

Rule: Less is more: fewer and simpler words make a stronger impact.

(a) **Original:** One may find that an accurate judgement about the contents of a printed publication cannot result from a cursory examination of the said publication's outer covering.

(b) **Revised:** The appearance of a book might not reflect its contents. *(Or, to repeat an old cliché: You can't tell a book by its cover.)*

Explanation: The original sentence (a) overstates an obvious idea for the sake of impressive-sounding language. Emphasis is lost, along with the reader's attention.

TIP 7: Vary sentence construction.

Rule: Vary sentence lengths and patterns. Keep the reader's attention tuned to your precise meanings and the emphasis you place on important ideas.

Example: Shakespeare's *Othello*

Cassio presents a different problem for Iago. Unlike Roderigo, Cassio is not stupid or immoral, but he does have a quick temper, a weak head for drink, and an extravagant concern for both courtesy and how others regard him. Where Roderigo seeks to satisfy his lust, Cassio longs for his reputation. (In fact, though Iago tries to provoke Cassio's desire for Desdemona, Cassio remains respectful to her at all times.) However, Iago, again in the guise of a good honest friend, will deceive Cassio by pretending to offer sound advice after he has created a situation to reverse his rival's fortunes.

Explanation: Note the use of varied sentence patterns in this passage. A short sentence introduces the subject. The second, longer sentence uses a list itemizing ideas to be developed. The third sentence creates a balance to show contrasting motives of two characters.

The long and the short of sentence construction

Use long sentences in these situations:

- to build word pictures
- to express ideas of equal importance in wording that gives equal weight to each thought (see parallelism in the next chapter on mechanics)
- to show the relationship between major and minor ideas

Use short sentences for emphasis:

- to accent an idea in the introduction
- to strengthen an existing link between subtopics
- to stress an abrupt contrast
- to clinch the conclusion

CHAPTER SEVEN

Mechanics: Correct common errors

The last stage before making the final clean copy requires careful attention to the mechanical details. So far, we've been more concerned about ideas and arguments - arranging and expressing them in the best possible way. Now it's time to proofread your essay for correct grammar, usage, spelling and punctuation.

GET A GRIP ON GRAMMAR

Even if you don't know the formal names for the parts of speech or the rules of correct grammar, there are several common mechanical faults you can quickly learn to spot and correct. Review the examples given for sentence faults, subject-verb agreement and correct pronoun reference, and eliminate similar errors from your own work.

If you need additional help with all the rules of grammar and usage, check a handbook of style and mechanics such as the *MLA Handbook* or *The Complete Idiot's Guide to Grammar and Style*.

Repair sentence faults

Four common sentence errors are considered major grammar faults: fused sentence, comma-splice, fragment and run-on sentence.

Fault (1): A **fused sentence** is one made up of two complete sentences, combined without proper punctuation or a joining word.

Fault (2): A **comma-splice** is the same error, but uses a comma to "splice" the join.

Corrections: Use one of the following methods to correct these two errors:

- Separate the two sentences by using a period and capital letter.
- Use a semicolon where the sentences are incorrectly joined, if the two ideas are closely related.
- Use an appropriate connecting word. Remember that "and," "but" and "or" join ideas of equal importance. Words like "while," "because," "who," "which" and "that" connect ideas of lesser importance to the main idea.
- Reduce one of the two sentences to a short descriptive phrase. Pay careful attention to placement of commas.

Example: Shakespeare's *Hamlet*

(a) **Original:** Hamlet's uncle is Claudius the King of Denmark he is the antagonist in the play's central conflict.

(b) **Revised:** Hamlet's uncle, Claudius, the King of Denmark, is the antagonist in the play's central conflict.

Explanation: Sentence (a) is a fused sentence. The revised sentence (b) uses the fourth method, reducing one of the original sentences to a descriptive phrase.

Fault (3): A **fragment** is a partial sentence, and should be avoided in formal essays.

Correction: Attach a fragment to a complete sentence. Or add what is necessary to make it a complete sentence in itself.

Example: F. Scott Fitzgerald's *The Great Gatsby*

(a) **Original:** Tom Buchanan pretends to be a loving father and dutiful husband. Although he has a mistress whom he sees frequently in New York City.

(b) **Revised:** Tom Buchanan, who has a mistress he sees frequently in New York City, pretends to be a loving father and dutiful husband.

Explanation: In the revised version (b), the fragment is attached as a description of the main subject, Tom Buchanan.

Fault (4): A **run-on sentence** contains too many ideas that are usually better expressed in shorter sentences.

Correction: Break a run-on construction into two or more short statements.

Example: Shakespeare's *Othello*

(a) **Original:** At first Iago works on Othello's good nature and trusting character by suggesting that his lieutenant, Cassio, is in love with Desdemona, and then he encourages Othello's jealousy by arranging a meeting between Cassio and Desdemona.

(b) **Revised:** At first Iago works on Othello's good nature and trusting character. After suggesting that Othello's lieutenant, Cassio, is in love with Desdemona, Iago encourages Othello's jealousy. He arranges a meeting between Cassio and Desdemona.

Explanation: In (a), one long sentence expresses four important ideas. Most readers will get lost in this pile of information. In the revised version (b), clarity is restored by dividing the main ideas among three sentences.

Ensure subject-verb agreement

Subject-verb agreement is based on whether the subject of a verb – the "doer" of an action – is singular or plural. It's usually obvious that a singular subject requires a singular verb form, and a plural subject requires a plural verb. However, watch for the following special situations.

Rule (1): Phrases using "with," "together with," "as well as" and "including" do not change a singular subject to plural.

Example: In Shakespeare's *Othello*, the protagonist, as well as several minor characters, is deceived by the villain Iago.

Rule (2): Compound subjects (two or more ideas with "and" as joining word) are plural. However, when a compound subject names one person, place or thing, the verb is singular.

Example: In Shakespeare's *Hamlet*, the chief councillor and co-conspirator of the king is an old man named Polonius.

Rule (3): When the parts of a compound subject are joined by "or" or "nor," the verb agrees with the nearer subject.

Example: In *Twelfth Night*, neither Sir Toby nor his friends are able to decide who is the real bridegroom.

Rule (4): A subject that is plural in form but names a single thing has a singular verb.

Example: Only ten months of the decade-long war at Troy is covered in Homer's epic poem, *The Iliad*.

Rule (5): "Each," "every," "neither," "one," "many a," "a person" and words ending in "-body" or "-one" take singular verbs.

Example: Everyone in the play *Much Ado about Nothing* knows that Beatrice and Benedick are in love.

Rule (6): A collective noun, such as "class," "crowd," "assembly," takes a singular verb when the group is considered, and a plural verb when the individuals who make up the group are thought of.

Example: The mob surrounding the guillotine cheers fiercely at every bloody execution in *A Tale of Two Cities*, Dickens' famous novel about the French Revolution.

Avoid ambiguous pronoun reference

Rule (1): Pronouns agree with their antecedents (the words they stand for) in number (singular or plural), gender (masculine, feminine or neuter) and person (first, second or third).

There is usually no problem with simple pronouns as long as you and the reader can clearly identify a specific antecedent for each one. Problems arise when singular and plural forms are used in the same sentence.

Example: Shakespeare's *Twelfth Night*

(a) **Original:** The <u>characters</u> find that <u>their</u> various mistakes are sorted out when Sebastian and Viola finally meet and <u>each</u> explains <u>their</u> part in the story.

(b) **Revised:** The <u>characters</u> find that <u>their</u> various mistakes are sorted out when Sebastian and Viola finally meet and <u>each</u> explains <u>his or her</u> part in the story.

Explanation: In (b), the antecedent of the plural form "their" is "characters." The antecedent of the singular possessive forms "his or her" is the word "each," meaning "each one" (singular).

Rule (2): Do not use a pronoun if there is doubt about its antecedent. Reword the sentence, or supply a needed noun.

Example: Shakespeare's *Twelfth Night*

(a) **Original:** Although <u>Antonio</u> rescues the young man <u>he</u> thinks is Sebastian, <u>he</u> is unaware of what is really going on.

(b) **Revised:** Although <u>Antonio</u> rescues the young man <u>he</u> thinks is Sebastian, <u>Antonio</u> is unaware of what is really going on.

Explanation: In sentence (a), the second pronoun "he" could refer to either "Antonio" or "Sebastian" as its antecedent. Sentence (b) clarifies the ambiguity.

Rule (3): The relative pronoun "which" relates or connects a less important idea to a specific word - its antecedent. "Which" must not be used to refer to a whole idea.

Example: Arthur Miller's *Death of a Salesman*

(a) **Original:** Willy Loman <u>is no longer able to cope</u> with the ways of modern business, <u>which</u> is the reason for the drastic action he takes to escape his problems.

(b) **Revised – adequate:**

Willy Loman is no longer able to cope with the ways of modern business. This <u>situation</u> causes him to take drastic action to escape his problems.

(c) **Revised – best:**

Because Willy Loman is no longer able to cope with the ways of modern business, he takes drastic action to escape his problems.

Explanation: In sentence (a), the word "which," according to the rule above, has "business" as its antecedent. This makes no sense. "Which" really refers to the idea expressed in the first part of the sentence: that Willy can no longer cope.

The revised version (b) is better. The word "situation" sums up the whole idea of the first sentence – an improvement over (a), but still not the best solution.

The sentence as revised in (c) correctly shows the relationship between the less important and more important ideas.

LOOK OUT FOR USAGE

Correct usage depends on familiarity with the special qualities of language – its peculiar idioms that often bend or ignore strict grammar rules.

Use consistent verb tenses

Rule: In writing narrative – i.e. telling a story of your own – use past tense consistently to relate the actions of characters. In essay writing, when you are analyzing some other writer's narrative, use present tense consistently, even to explain plot incidents that have occurred in the past.

Examples: Hugh Garner's "One, Two, Three Little Indians"

(a) From the short story:

When he <u>reached</u> the shanty he <u>opened</u> the door and <u>fell</u> inside. He <u>placed</u> the body of his son on the bed in the corner. Then, groping around the newspaper-lined walls, he <u>found</u> some matches in a pocket of his mackinaw and <u>lit</u> the lamp.

(b) From a student essay analyzing this story:

At the climax of his short story "One, Two, Three Little Indians," Garner creates a mood of despair by describing Tom's simple activities as he places his dead infant on the bed and lights the only lamp.

Explanation: In (a), Garner uses verbs in the past tense to tell his story: "reached," "opened," "fell," "placed," found," "lit." In (b), the student writer expresses some of the same actions, but uses present tense for verbs: "creates," "places," "lights."

Beware of faulty parallelism

Parallelism means two or more parts of a sentence are similar in construction, importance and relation to the rest of the statement. In other words, these parts look the same, carry the same weight and relate to the rest of the sentence in the same way.

Rule: Express ideas of equal importance in parallel form.

Example: Shakespeare's *Macbeth*

(a) **Original:** The Weird Sisters in *Macbeth* speak of Macbeth's present success, his future advancement, and how he must beware the Thane of Fife.

(b) **Revised:** The Weird Sisters in *Macbeth* speak of Macbeth's present success, his future advancement, and his ultimate need for caution regarding the Thane of Fife.

Explanation: Sentence (a) has three parts that should be parallel. The nouns "success" and "advancement" are parallel, but the third element, "how he must beware the Thane of Fife," is not. Sentence (b) replaces this part with a noun, "need," and adds a descriptive word, "ultimate," thus creating correct parallelism.

Parallel structure is a sophisticated way to create sentences in which ideas can be clearly stated and related to each other, and emphasis carefully controlled.

Looking for parallels

- Parallelism is especially useful in your introduction for identifying the subtopics you intend to develop.
- As a stylistic device, parallelism, used correctly, is a clever way to construct clear sentences and create emphasis. Make parallelism part of your mature style.
- Check parallel structure by trying the two or more parallel elements in a vertical layout like this:

  The Weird Sisters in *Macbeth* speak of
  - Macbeth's present success
  - his future advancement
  - his ultimate need for caution

PERFECT YOUR SPELLING

There are many rules and tricky rhymes (known as mnemonics) or other devices that appeal to spelling experts. The problem is that English has too many exceptions for every rule. A good dictionary is still the best authority. Memorize the words you frequently misspell.

Watch out for these non-existent words

alot	irregardless
alright	mischievious
anyways	preplan
inflammable	prophecize

SORT OUT YOUR PUNCTUATION

Punctuation is necessary for clear expression. In the rules and examples below, we'll concentrate on special uses that you may need in writing a senior English essay. For complete details, consult the style and mechanics text such as *MLA Handbook*, or *The Complete Idiot's Guide to Grammar and Style*.

Separate with the semicolon

Rule (1): Use semicolons between items in a series when one or more of those items contain commas. This semicolon construction is useful for introducing parallel subtopics in a thesis statement.

Example: Nick Carraway serves three purposes in *The Great Gatsby*: as an innocent observer, marvelling at Gatsby's excesses; as a commentator, moralizing over his death; and as a narrator, telling the story from a consistent point of view.

Rule (2): Use a semicolon between complete statements closely related in thought when there is no conjunction or joining word.

Example: The narrator is from the Midwest; he returns there after Gatsby's death.

Insert with parentheses

Rule (1): Use parentheses to enclose an "aside" - extra information or an explanation that is not essential to the sentence.

Example: The main characters in modern drama (for example, Willy and Biff in *Death of a Salesman*) often reflect in their lives the larger issues and conflicts of their society.

Rule (2): Use parentheses in your essay for references that direct the reader to sources noted in your bibliography. (For correct form of such in-text citations, see chapter 9.)

Example: At the end of Joseph Conrad's *Heart of Darkness*, Marlow is isolated from his listeners, sitting "in the pose of a meditating Buddha" (Conrad 131).

Clarify with brackets

Rule: Use brackets to show a change or addition you've made for the sake of clarity in a quotation from a primary or secondary source. (See chapter 9 for details.)

Example: In her commentary on the Canadian short story "The Father," Eva Taube says, "The author [Hugh Garner] portrays a man, who, like many a conformist, is defensive and insecure."

Interrupt with the dash

Rule: Use a dash to emphasize an interruption in a sentence, or a sudden change of direction in a thought. **Note**: Don't confuse a dash with a simple hyphen. A hyphen is used in spelling many two-part words such as *well-known*, and to show a syllable break at the end of a line of text.

Example: In Ray Bradbury's *Fahrenheit 451*, the reasons for Guy Montag's breakdown - and there are many - come from his disillusionment with his world.

Quote titles with quotation marks

Rule: Use double quotation marks to enclose titles of short stories, short plays, poems, essays and chapter headings - that is, titles of pieces that are normally published as parts of a collection.

Note that titles of separately published works - novels, full-length plays and anthologies - are shown in italics (or underlined on a typewriter).

Examples:

(a) "The Yellow Sweater" is a famous Canadian short story by Hugh Garner. It appears in a paperback collection called *Hugh Garner's Best Stories*.

(b) A typical senior English essay title might be, "The King's Henchmen in Shakespeare's *Hamlet*."

The other uses for quotation marks - quoting from sources as supporting evidence in your essay - are covered in chapter 9.

PROOFREADING: SAMPLE ESSAY-IN-PROGRESS

Study the corrections in this essay-in-progress on Shakespeare's *Hamlet*. Note the improvements in all three areas - substance, style and mechanics. Use this as a model for proofreading and correcting your essay before making the fair copy.

The King's Henchmen in Shakespeare's *Hamlet*	**Style/Mechanics Notes**
In Shakespeare's *Hamlet*, T ~~t~~he tragedy that engulfs most of the major and secondary characters results from the conflict between	*Reword for more emphatic opening*
the ~~two~~ chief opponents, Hamlet and Claudius. Among the secondary	*Deadwood*
characters, Polonius, Rosencrantz, ~~and~~ Guildenstern, and Laertes are clearly victims in that conflict, though not necessarily innocent ones.	*Awkward*
Assessing how responsible each of them is for ~~their~~ his own death	*Faulty pronoun agreement (antecedent* <u>*each*</u> *is singular)*
depends on the extent of their involvement in the conflict, ~~there~~ his own motives and ~~how they die.~~ the manner of his death.	*Faulty parallelism (3 nouns: involvement, motives, manner)*
~~Reviewing~~ Polonius' ~~role in the play reveals how he~~ is almost	*Deadwood*
completely responsible for his own death. Since he beleives believes he is	*Wrong spelling*
doing ~~the~~ right ~~thing~~ in trying to help ~~Prince~~ Hamlet, he thinks	*Deadwood/cliché*
nothing of using ~~and exploiting~~ his own daughter to help the King	*Deadwood/repetition*
spy on the prince ~~Hamlet. We see this in~~ In the so-called "nunnery scene,"	*No " " needed with* <u>*so-called*</u>
~~when~~ Polonius and Claudius hide behind a wall-hanging, ~~in order~~ to	*Deadwood*
eavesdrop on the meeting they've they have arranged between Hamlet and	*Avoid contraction*
Ophelia. ~~As~~ Hamlet soon figures out the situation, and he treats Ophelia badly.	*Awkward*
None of this, however, changes Polonius' wrong idea about the	*Apostrophe for possessive*
relationship between the prince and Ophelia. ~~d~~ D espite Claudius' quite different reaction, Polonius arranges another eavesdropping scene	*Comma-splice*
in Gertrude's chamber. When Hamlet rashly kills the old man, he sums up Polonius' fate in these dismissive words: "Thou find'st to be	*Apostrophe for possessives and for contraction*
too busy is ~~a~~ some danger" (III.4.33).	*Quote accurately*

LEARN FROM YOUR MISTAKES

There are lots of ways to chart your own progress as you go through two or three school years of senior English. The "look-out" log and grammar error chart shown here are popular with some teachers. Keep these in your English notebook or classroom writing portfolio, or create and save them in a computer file, perhaps on the disk where you store all your writing samples, research notes, works-in-progress and finished essays.

Consult and update your logs regularly. Make a serious effort to improve on your own common errors.

Spelling Demons: Look Out!

Assignment/Date	Correct Spelling
Henchman Jan. 10	*believe* ~~*beleive*~~

Grammar problems:
Error correction chart

Assignment / Date	Error
Henchman Jan. 10	*pronoun agreement*
Correction	*each (sing) followed by his*
Correction	
Correction	
Correction	
Correction	
Correction	
Correction	

Spelling problems
Your computer won't catch

Spell-check programs cannot distinguish between sound-alike words (homonyms) if they're spelled correctly. Even recent grammar programs may miss tricky spelling decisions.

Watch especially for these and know which spelling you need:

already - all ready
altogether - all together
cite - sight - site
everyday - every day
for - four - fore
hear - here
hole - whole
passed - past
principal - principle
right - write - wright
there - their - they're
threw - through
to - too - two
weather - whether

CHECK THE MARKING CRITERIA

Here's a typical teacher checklist for marking a senior English essay. Many teachers provide a blank form such as this one with the assignment to show the marking criteria.

Use this as a checklist as you revise and polish your work in progress, and as a score card to evaluate your finished essay.

Senior Literary Essay

Title . . . . Date . . . . Mark . . . . /20

Substance . . . . /10	**Style** . . . . /3	**Mechanics** . . . . /4
❑ Interesting introduction	❑ Individual "voice"	❑ Grammar
❑ Freshness of thought	❑ Appropriate language level	❑ Usage
❑ Insight offered	❑ Clarity of expression	❑ Spelling
❑ Adequate supporting material	❑ Conciseness	❑ Punctuation
❑ Sufficient detail	❑ Fluency	
❑ Convincing conclusion		

Organization – CUE. . . . . /3

Coherence	**Unity**	**Emphasis**
❑ Clear plan	❑ Clear focus	❑ Thesis statement
❑ Correct paragraphing	❑ On topic	❑ Forceful restatement
❑ Links and transitions	❑ Relevant subtopics	
❑ Appropriate development	❑ Supporting evidence	
❑ Supporting evidence		

Comment ____

____

____

____

CHAPTER EIGHT

The in-class and examination essay

A senior English examination is usually one and a half to two hours in length. It may consist of just one section and a single task – to write an essay of 700-800 words, given a choice of two or more questions. Well-prepared students know how to use the available time efficiently. They spend the first 10–15 minutes reading and analyzing the chosen question, and create a simple, point-form outline, using some version of the template shown in chapter 2.

Most students come to a senior English examination well prepared. They usually know the content of the literary work the essay question will deal with. But what distinguishes an above-average essay from an average effort? An A student knows how to *select* from the store of knowledge, and how to *organize* that material into a coherent and logical essay. What's important is not how much you know, but how you use what you know.

That's what teachers are looking for: an appropriate selection of ideas and evidence in response to a given question, and a logical presentation of those materials. Careful selection and organization are the keys to an A essay.

Pre-test prep

While studying and preparing for an in-class or examination essay:

- Check with your teacher: Is it an open-book test? Is a "cheat-sheet" of prepared notes allowed? Are printed or electronic dictionaries permitted in the exam room?
- Don't mark up your school text. Instead, pick up a cheap, second-hand copy of the text and use a highlighter pen. Fill the margins with useful notes and commentary.
- Create a memory-work log of words, phrases and short passages of important material in the primary text and memorize these ahead of time.
- For a test/essay on Shakespeare, focus on soliloquies and other major speeches.
- Check your school library for filed copies of old exams. Look for Coles Notes that have sample questions and answers. Ask your teacher for a page of review questions and examination hints.
- Don't miss the teacher's in-class exam review on context, format and marking scheme. Now create your own exam as a final review exercise.

PLAY IT SAFE ON IN-CLASS AND EXAMINATION ESSAYS

For an in-class essay question or assignment, don't take risks: use the given subject and its limits, and follow the arrangement suggested by the question itself.

Time constraints make this a logical approach. You've no doubt had the experience (or known other students who have had it) of running out of time because you spent too long trying to revise and rearrange the given question, instead of writing and revising on a plan already suggested by the teacher.

Taking risks also relates to the style you choose for expressing ideas. On an in-class or examination essay, content usually outweighs style in the marking scheme. Use simple, declarative sentences and familiar vocabulary, especially when time for dictionary-browsing is limited.

Analyze a model essay

The following essay on Shakespeare's *Othello* is a response to a typical senior English examination question, and reflects A-level work. **Note:** You don't have to know details of the plot to follow the process for constructing a thesis as shown here.

For each essay section - introduction, body, conclusion - the box on the left itemizes the content. The commentary boxes provide a teacher's assessment of the strengths and weaknesses of each section, focusing on substance and structure.

Mechanical errors have been eliminated, since teachers expect senior English students to write error-free prose, without serious problems in grammar, usage, spelling and punctuation.

Sample Question and model Essay on Shakespeare's **Othello**

To set his shrewd schemes in motion, Iago relies heavily on his ability to exploit the human weaknesses, or even the virtues, of Roderigo, Cassio and Othello. Identify three such traits for each character, and assess how each flaw or factor contributes to the downfall of each victim.

Commentary on Question

This assisted essay question supplies the limited subject - Iago's exploitation of human weaknesses - but requires that the student identify three traits for each of the three characters named.

Draft outline: Examination essay on Othello

The following outline takes 10 minutes to prepare. It provides just enough structure to suggest supporting evidence and keep the essay logically organized.

Introduction

Broad subject: **Shakespeare's tragedy *Othello***

Limited subject: **Iago's exploitation of human weaknesses and virtues**

Thesis statement: In William Shakespeare's tragic play *Othello*, Iago's evil schemes deceive Roderigo, Cassio and Othello until after tragedy strikes. Iago manipulates all three victims by successfully exploiting a different set of weaknesses or even virtues in each man's personality.

Body: Part 1
Development

Subtopic A
with supporting
evidence:

Roderigo: 3 traits

(1) lust

(2) self-doubt

(3) indecisiveness

Body: Part 2
Development

Subtopic B
with supporting
evidence:

Cassio: 3 traits

(1) quick temper

(2) weak head for drink

(3) concern for courtesy and reputation

Body: Part 3
Development

Subtopic C
with supporting
evidence:

Othello: 3 traits

(1) trusting nature

(2) social insecurity

(3) military decisiveness

Conclusion – Reinforcement of thesis

Roderigo, Cassio and Othello are the unwitting and tragic victims of Iago's evil schemes. None of the three sees through Iago's deceit until tragedy strikes in the form of Desdemona's murder. . .

MODEL ESSAY: SHAKESPEARE'S OTHELLO

Introduction:
38 words/2 sentences

- author and title are cited
- limited subject is specified: Iago's exploitation of human weaknesses
- subtopics are noted – three victims identified: Roderigo, Cassio, Othello

In William Shakespeare's tragic play *Othello*, Iago's evil schemes deceive Roderigo, Cassio and Othello until after tragedy strikes. Iago manipulates all three victims by successfully exploiting a different set of weaknesses or even virtues in each man's personality.

Body – Paragraph 1:
Subtopic A: Roderigo
195 words/9 sentences

- first sentence ("mini-thesis") introduces subtopic A: Roderigo as victim
- specific traits of Roderigo's character are itemized: lust, self-doubt, indecisiveness
- brief plot references illustrate these three weaknesses

Iago plays upon Roderigo's weaknesses: his lust, his self-doubt, and his inability to make up his mind. Though an ardent and longtime suitor of Desdemona, Roderigo never encounters her during the play. He does not act upon his lustful feelings. Instead, he readily allows Iago to manage the affair, threatening to approach Desdemona only after Iago strips him of all his money. However, Iago is able to redirect Roderigo each time because Roderigo, in his self-doubt, is reluctant to take charge of any situation and is too unimaginative to do so even if he had the will. When defeat looms, Roderigo either retreats or contemplates suicide. He cannot make up his own mind, and it is Iago who supplies the energy, the hope, the reassurances and the schemes to keep Roderigo involved in the plot for revenge. Iago's final leverage is the argument that he is honest and caring. Roderigo is foolish enough to believe this even after hearing Iago declare early on, "I am not what I am." In summary, Roderigo's lust spurs him on while his self-doubt and indecisiveness ensure that Iago remains firmly in the saddle with his hands on the reins.

Commentary *Introduction*

Brevity: This introduction is a straightforward restatement of the given examination question, and contains all the necessary elements. The introduction is kept short because of the time constraints in an exam situation. The specific traits of each character are stated in the opening sentences of each subtopic.

Subtopic order: Subtopics are given in the order they appear in the question. The logical sequence is from least important to most important character. There is no reason to change this.

Unity: This student suggests a unifying link for the three characters with the phrase "until after tragedy strikes." This implies that Iago's three victims have something in common: each is ignorant of Iago's scheming until it is too late. This idea goes beyond what the given question requires, providing an additional unifying point. It anticipates an emphatic restatement in the conclusion.

Coherence: This introduction, though brief, provides the solid framework expected of an A essay. The outline on the previous page allows the student to work quickly and efficiently through the formula for each subtopic – a no-risk approach that is right for an examination.

Commentary *Body: Subtopic A – Roderigo*

Opening: The first sentence, which introduces this subtopic's mini-thesis, provides a skilful link to the essay's main thesis, by repeating both the word "weaknesses," and the idea of Iago's manipulation of those weaknesses (in the phrase "plays upon").

Coherence: Several internal links, such as "instead" and "however," sustain coherence within the paragraph.

Emphasis: Iago's exploitation of Roderigo is emphasized throughout with phrases such as "able to redirect Roderigo," "supplies . . . the schemes to keep Roderigo involved" and "Iago's final leverage."

Supporting evidence: Brief references are made to plot incidents, such as Roderigo's contemplation of suicide in Act I, scene 3. As well, a brief, relevant quotation is used in supporting the description of Iago's character. The quotation emphasizes the irony in the way Iago victimizes Roderigo while appearing to be an honest friend.

Closing: The final sentence unifies this paragraph. It begins with a link, "In summary," and does in fact summarize ideas about the three weaknesses in Roderigo's character that have been explained and illustrated.

Body (cont.) –
Paragraph 2:
Subtopic B: Cassio
257 words/13 sentences

- first two sentences introduce subtopic B: Cassio as victim
- specific traits, both weaknesses and virtues, are itemized: quick temper, weak head for drink, concern for courtesy and reputation
- specific references to several incidents appear as supporting evidence

Cassio presents a different problem for Iago. Unlike Roderigo, Cassio is not stupid or immoral, but he does have a quick temper, a weak head for drink and an extravagant concern for both courtesy and how others regard him. Where Roderigo seeks to satisfy his lust, Cassio longs for his reputation. (In fact, though Iago tries to provoke Cassio's desire for Desdemona, Cassio remains respectful to her at all times.) However, Iago, again in the guise of a good honest friend, will deceive Cassio by pretending to offer sound advice after he has created a situation to reverse his rival's fortunes. Iago is able to induce Cassio to drink the disastrous cup of wine because Cassio wants to be pleasant to Iago's friends. Soon after, Cassio's quick temper and drunken state allow Roderigo to draw him into a quarrel. Later, Cassio's gallantry first prompts him to ask Bianca to copy the strawberry handkerchief design and then prevents him from publicly arguing with her after she accuses him of taking a new lover. This admirably serves Iago's purpose. Cassio now appears to be Desdemona's lover. Meanwhile, Othello works himself into a jealous fury as he overhears and misconstrues the exchange between Iago, Cassio and Bianca. Thus, Cassio's temper, along with his inability to remain sober on a small amount of wine, gives Iago the opportunity to exploit his chief weakness - the concern that others think well of him, a desire which is at once virtue and vanity. In these three qualities, Iago finds the means to manipulate Cassio.

Commentary *Body: Subtopic B – Cassio*

Opening: In linking this subtopic to the previous one, and to the essay's main thesis, the writer establishes a contrast between Cassio and Roderigo. This is important, for it is Cassio's virtues as well as his weaknesses that Iago is able to exploit. The writer makes another link to the preceding paragraph with the word "guise," to emphasize once again that Iago is not what he seems.

Coherence: The writer sets us up for his third subtopic, by previewing here Othello's reaction to the deceptive scene arranged by Iago. Thus, this paragraph looks back to the weakness of Roderigo that Iago exploited, and ahead to the third subtopic about the manipulation of Othello.

Supporting evidence: Several specific plot incidents are mentioned in support of the idea summed up in the phrase that concludes this subtopic: "Iago finds the means to manipulate Cassio."

Closing: The final sentence also unifies this paragraph by suggesting again that Cassio is exploited through both weaknesses and virtues.

Body (cont.) –
Paragraph 3:
Subtopic C: Othello
216 words/11 sentences

- first three sentences establish subtopic C: the victimization of Othello
- specific traits of Othello's character are explained: trusting nature, social insecurity, military decisiveness
- specific references to several incidents appear as supporting evidence

Iago's toughest challenge is Othello, for the commander's trusting nature and decisiveness as a military leader are more strengths than weaknesses. Iago is aware, however, of Othello's insecurity as a foreigner among the ruling class of Venice. And here again Iago falls back on his outward appearance as an honest, trustworthy friend to win Othello's confidence. Iago begins to corrupt Othello by abusing his open and trusting nature. Next, he attempts to exploit Othello's social insecurity as a racial and cultural foreigner to Venice by raising the question of whether it is natural that Desdemona would not "affect many proposed matches / Of her own clime, perfection and degree." (It is a measure of Othello's greatness that Iago never completely succeeds with this ploy.) To arouse Othello, Iago does not focus on concerns for reputation as he did with Cassio. The fact that Othello might be known as a cuckold is not the main reason Iago's lies about Desdemona inflame the general. Rather Othello is made distraught because his trust and fundamental vision of good are shredded. Once Othello is aroused, Iago engineers the tragedy by relying on the general's military decisiveness and ability to take action. Iago thus exploits Othello's strengths, bringing him close to madness and providing a motive for the military commander to act.

Commentary *Subtopic C – Othello*

Opening: The introduction of the third subtopic is not as explicit as were the previous ones. The writer points out that Iago must exploit strengths as well as weaknesses in his third victim. Here, the writer relies on our understanding of the logical plan, to emphasize Iago's underhanded methods in abusing his commander's character.

Coherence: Link words and phrases include "here again," "then," "next." The word "exploit" repeats the idea already clearly established in "plays upon" in the first subtopic, and "manipulate" in the second. Both "exploit" and "manipulate" are links to the introduction as well. A brief reference to Cassio's concern for reputation provides a link to the previous paragraph.

Supporting evidence and emphasis: The quotation about Desdemona emphasizes an important idea, that Iago is capable of seeing and exploiting a weakness in Othello that is not at first apparent, his social insecurity, an awareness of being somewhat out of place in Venetian society.

Closing: The final statement about Iago relying on Othello to take action and "bring about tragedy" indicates the villain's role in the play's tragic climax, the murder of Desdemona.

Conclusion:
108 words/6 sentences

- three subtopics repeated in opening sentence
- brief quotation from the play's tragic conclusion sums up Iago's character
- the controlling idea, Iago's exploitation of his victims' human qualities, is reinforced
- a universal truth – the influence of evil in human life – concludes the essay

Totals:
814 words/41 sentences

Roderigo, Cassio and Othello are the unwitting and tragic victims of Iago's evil schemes. None of the three sees through Iago's deceit until tragedy strikes in the form of Desdemona's murder. The "demi-devil," as Othello calls Iago when everything is at last revealed, refuses to explain his actions. Perhaps he exploited his victims' weaknesses and virtues simply to fulfil his own evil nature. In this sense, "honest Iago" is in fact honest in being true to his own evil character. Appearances are deceiving, and Iago's methods of deception show how the devil can tragically exploit the human qualities in the strongest as well as the weakest among us.

Commentary *Conclusion*

Opening: The conclusion begins by counter-balancing the introduction with a terse review of the subtopics in the order they appeared in the body of the essay.

CUE:
Coherence
Unity
Emphasis
Coherence and unity are achieved with links to the introduction: repetition of key words such as "manipulate," "victims" and "weaknesses." An additional link is clearly established in the phrase, "until tragedy strikes," borrowed from the introduction. Two brief quotations, descriptive tags that apply to Iago's character, contribute to the essay's unity, the central focus on Iago's character and actions. They emphasize his role by summarizing his actions as described throughout the subtopics: his evil reality hiding beneath a false appearance of honesty and truth, as he exploits the weaknesses of others.

Arrangement: The ideas here move from the specific (the exploitation of Roderigo, Cassio and Othello) to the general (the influence of evil in human lives).

Closing: Finally, this conclusion provides a "clincher," an important idea about human nature, based on a familiar turn of phrase: "Appearances are deceiving."

CHAPTER NINE

The major independent essay

It may be called a "formal research essay," a "major term paper" or simply an "independent project." Whatever it's called, the independent essay is the goal for which earlier assignments - essays on examinations and as take-home exercises - prepare you.

The independent essay may range from 700 to 2,000 words, depending on how long you are given to complete the assignment, and what percentage of your term mark the teacher assigns for the project. Expectations about requirements for research in secondary sources may vary.

However, your finished independent essay will incorporate all the main features you've read about here: a well-developed thesis and the necessary supporting evidence; an objective, formal style; and careful attention to details of mechanics and formatting in the final fair copy.

In this chapter, we'll focus on four tasks:

- limiting the subject by choosing and narrowing your focus
- taking a stand to formulate a workable thesis statement
- researching the subject to establish your direction
- using research materials correctly and credibly in the essay

In the Appendix, we'll sample a senior independent essay that uses a "point-counterpoint" comparison method to examine two novels. You'll find there a demonstration of everything explained in this book.

LAUNCH YOUR ESSAY

Some teachers may provide in-class or private conference time to help you clarify your ideas before you get too far in the research and writing stages. Before starting, find out just how much help you may need and can expect. Come prepared and on time to any conference appointments. A portion of your assignment mark is usually given for your log-keeping activities and the conference itself.

Limit the subject

Methods in choosing a subject for a senior independent essay project may vary. Some teachers provide a reading list of novels, plays, stories, poems and essays related to your English course. Students explore materials of interest, then narrow their focus and construct a workable thesis on the author and work selected. Other teachers prefer to give students more help getting started. They provide a list of approved topics, with varying degrees of detail. Students choose a topic, then develop a manageable thesis statement.

Sample modern novel project

One high school uses the following set of instructions to accompany a senior independent essay project on a list of novels:

From the list of approved novels, reserve a specific title (alternative titles may be approved by the teacher). Make an appointment for a writing conference with the teacher. Then complete the following checklist in preparation:

- ❑ Read the entire novel, and choose a topic. While reading, note passages where the author's treatment of the topic or theme is significant.
- ❑ Reread and reflect. Refine the topic into a debatable thesis.
- ❑ Maintain a reading journal. Enter at least eight dated log notations, recording progress in developing the thesis. Respond to key passages in the novel, noting ideas for developing subtopics, and outlining questions for clarification.
- ❑ Locate critical commentaries (secondary sources) on the novel, the author and the social context (if relevant).

- ❑ Prepare a rough, point-form outline for the essay, with notes about supporting evidence from both primary and secondary sources.
- ❑ Prepare to discuss the author and novel, as well as your log entries, thesis, outline and sources.

A percentage of your final mark is usually awarded for preliminary activities such as those listed above. The teacher's conference notes, and early drafts of your essay, with evidence of revision and editing, may be included as well. Sometimes an oral presentation in class - not just a reading of the essay - is also a requirement, and part of the overall evaluation. See our Coles Notes book: *How to Get an A in School Projects and Presentations*.

Take a stand

State your thesis on the chosen subject in such a way that the reader can agree or disagree. In other words, stake out your ground and prepare to defend it.

Avoid a bland, "no-risk" thesis. The following, although suitable for a typical short essay question, is not controversial or debatable enough for an independent project.

Example: In Arthur Miller's *Death of a Salesman,* Linda is a problem character. It is unclear throughout the play whether she makes any honest attempt to save Willy from himself, or contributes to his downfall.

Revised: In Arthur Miller's *Death of a Salesman*, Linda actively contributes to Willy's tragedy by sheltering him, by ignoring his faults and by encouraging his distorted view of what success is.

This revised version is better because the student is now prepared to support one side of the debate about Linda's role in the play.

A student who can establish a strong position and support it convincingly has laid the groundwork for an A paper.

Open and close with the big picture

*For an independent essay of some length, divide your introduction into **two** paragraphs.*

- Ease the reader into your subject by placing it in a larger context. Think of the establishing shot that opens a movie, setting the scene for what follows.
- In the second shorter paragraph, present your thesis succinctly. Focus on the controlling idea and preview your subtopics.

In your conclusion, use two paragraphs again, and reverse the procedure.

- The second-last paragraph of the essay reviews subtopics to reinforce the controlling idea.
- The final short paragraph leaves the reader with something to think about - how your thesis applies to the world beyond your limited subject.

RESEARCH THE SUBJECT

Make efficient notes

Making useful notes from both primary and secondary sources can be an art in itself. Using 3″ x 5″ index cards, available from any office supply store, is still a good method. Small index cards have three advantages over notebook pages:

- They force you to focus on your subject and on subtopics of manageable size.
- They restrict the amount of space (and time) you use in making notes.
- They provide an easily organized source for preparing your reference list.

Miller, Arthur, *Death of a Salesman* card 3 of 6

Miller, Arthur, *Death of a Salesman* card 2 of 6

Miller, Arthur, *Death of a Salesman* card 1 of 6

Certain private conversations in two acts and a requiem.
New York: Viking Press. 1949.

page 35 - Willy: "Because the man who makes an appearance in the business world, the man who creates personal interest, is the man who gets ahead. Be liked and you will never want."

- Willy living in the past when being "well-liked" could still sell merchandise

- doesn't understand changes in society and in his own business

Use your note cards in this way:

- Record author, title and complete publication information of any work consulted (including the primary source) on a separate card. Do this first! You'll need it for formal papers.
- As you record notes and quotes on additional cards, use a short-form title or author name at the top of each new card. Number the cards consecutively.
- Keep each bundle of cards separate - one primary or secondary source per bundle.
- Use a highlighter pen for marking important ideas, quotations and problems on your cards. Add brief references about these to your working log, and discuss them with your teacher or writing partners.

RESEARCH THE SUBJECT

Establish your direction

Literary essays may take different directions. One type looks inward, at the substance of a particular work and its unique features and writing techniques. A second type looks outward from the work, to examine its social context. Here's where secondary sources can help.

An example of the first approach is the sample essay on *Othello* in chapter 8. The student writer focuses on characters and their relationships with each other. There's almost no reference to anything outside the plot.

The second approach requires a more sophisticated understanding of how literature relates to real life. Exploring an author's work in relation to the social context in which he works can provide excellent topics and thesis ideas for a senior independent project. For example, an independent essay on *Macbeth* might examine attitudes and beliefs about witchcraft in Shakespeare's time.

Know your sources

Sources for research are of two kinds:

- **Primary source** refers to the particular literary work your essay is about - the poem, play, short story, novel or essay that you are analyzing.
- **Secondary sources** are relevant materials prepared by someone other than your chosen author. Commentaries and analyses relating to your subject are available as published books and articles.

Armed with your topic and your index cards, head for the library. As you consult sources, keep the following in mind:

- In establishing your direction, the "general to specific" pattern works as well in research as it does in structuring an essay. Start with reference works. Get a broad overview of your author and his or her work.
- Don't get bogged down in details. Back off: explore the subject in a larger context before closing in.
- Try beginning with a junior text that covers relevant social issues. The less sophisticated treatment quickly establishes context. Then move to more mature materials with confidence.

When you're ready to take a stand and formulate your thesis, follow these suggestions:

- Review your note cards when you're not in the library. Look for recurring ideas - themes, literary techniques, social context - that might support your thesis.
- Have one or more preliminary versions of a thesis ready for your teacher conference.
- Once your subject and controlling idea are set, go back to secondary sources for more materials before starting the raw draft of your essay.

Questions to ask

Begin by reviewing your primary source(s). Then move to secondary sources as noted below.

Use these questions to guide your research:

- What are the major themes your author treats in other writings?
- What other writers cover similar subjects or themes?
- What narrative or dramatic techniques is your author known for?
- How important an influence is the contemporary social and historical context in your author's work?

Where to look

Work through as many of the sources listed below as time permits.

1. Starting out

Library:

Dictionaries	Encyclopedias
Handbooks of literature	Periodical indexes
Literary journals	Electronic media: videos / CD-ROMs

Classroom:

Text/Introduction	Class notes/Handouts
Teacher conference	Class discussion

Online / Internet:

Title/Author search

2. Closing in

Biographies	Other works by author
Social/Historical context	

3. Getting specific

Annotated editions	Anthologies of criticism
Study guides (e.g., Coles Notes)	Monographs

USE RESEARCH MATERIALS CORRECTLY

Paraphrase, quote, cite the source

As you write your raw draft and work through several revisions to your finished version, learn to use material from secondary sources correctly. There are several general rules you need to know about paraphrasing, quoting and acknowledging the sources of such materials.

1. **Cite sources within your essay text:** Name your source as you introduce a paraphrase or quotation used as supporting evidence. Then the correct acknowledgement of your source need be only a page reference in parentheses at the end of the sentence or paragraph. This is called an in-text citation, and is preferred over the older footnoting method. The in-text style is fully demonstrated in the *MLA Handbook*.

2. **Paraphrase a passage:** Restate ideas from a primary or a secondary source in your own words. Avoid any distinctive wording as found in the source. If key words or phrases are unavoidable, show them in quotation marks.

3. **Quote a passage:** Keep quotations short, and quote accurately. Be sure to indicate, clearly and in correct form, any changes you make to the original. Conventions for correctly using quoted material are explained in the next section.

4. **Don't plagiarize:** Plagiarism is a serious charge. Never present someone else's ideas as your own! Originality in your essay derives from how well you do the following:

   - present your stand
   - explain and illustrate your ideas
   - use secondary support - paraphrase or quotation, correctly acknowledged

Borrowing ideas from a secondary source is okay, but borrowing actual words requires the correct use of quotation marks. In either case, you must acknowledge the source of the borrowed material.

To quote or not to quote?

Use direct quotations sparingly. Some students think that padding an essay with lots of quotations makes it more impressive as a piece of scholarly writing. In fact, the opposite is true: the more padding, the less credit you will get for originality, and for adequately developing and supporting the thesis.

When should you quote? When a paraphrase doesn't seem strong enough. A quotation is most effective when the passage quoted is particularly unusual or interesting. Remember, every quotation is an interruption in the flow of your own writing style. Choose quotes that are especially meaningful and memorable.

QUOTATION CONVENTIONS

When you quote, follow these rules. Each rule is illustrated on the following pages.

1. **All quotations:** Quote accurately, word-for-word, comma-for-comma. These three common changes in the form or content of a quotation are allowed:

- Show any omission from the quoted passage with an ellipsis: three spaced periods (. . .), but don't leave out any relevant parts of the quote. (Use four spaced periods if the part omitted includes the end of a sentence.) *See example (c).*
- If you add emphasis with italics or underlining that is not in the original, use a bracketed note at the end of the quote [emphasis added]. *See example (e).*
- Show any addition to the quoted passage in brackets [ ]. *See example (f).*

2. **Short quotations:** Keep most quotations brief - a word or phrase, up to a maximum of four lines of continuous prose or three lines of verse.

- Weave short quotations into carefully constructed sentences to ensure grammatical accuracy. *See examples (b), (c), (e) and (f).*

- Use double quotation marks around the actual words you quote. Use single quotation marks for any quotation marks that appear in the original source. *See example (f).*
- Place the in-text citation in parentheses at the end of the passage containing the quote, *before* the sentence period. *See examples (a) to (h).*
- Follow the same style for short verse quotations, but use a diagonal (/) to show line breaks. Retain any capital letters that appear in the source. *See example (i).*

3. **Long quotations:** If you must use a longer quotation (more than four lines of prose, three lines of verse), set it off from the text of your essay. *See examples (g) and (j).*

- Start a new line and indent 2.5 cm (one inch) (10 typed spaces) to the right of the left margin.
- For verse quotation, reproduce any unusual spacing between words as it appears in the original.
- Do not use quotation marks at beginning and end. Quotation marks that appear in the original must be retained. *See example (g).*
- Place the in-text citation in parentheses *after* the end punctuation. (Note how this differs from normal usage for short quotations.)
- Double-space a set-off quotation like the rest of your essay.

Here's how: Paraphrasing, quoting and citing sources

The 10 examples in this section are from a student essay on nonsense in children's literature. Each example shows one or more applications of the rules for correct paraphrasing, quoting and citing sources, as explained in the previous section.

Study each example and its explanation carefully. Then use these models as your guide when handling source material in your own essay. Incorporating a variety of methods for paraphrasing and quoting is an essential feature of an A paper.

Source material: *The first three examples of paraphrase and quotation draw on this passage from Bruno Bettelheim's psychological study of the importance of fairy tales,* The Uses of Enchantment.

Like all great art, fairy tales both delight and instruct; their special genius is that they do so in terms which speak directly to children. At the age when these stories are most meaningful to the child, his major problem is to bring some order into the inner chaos of his mind so that he can understand himself better – a necessary preliminary for achieving some congruence between his perceptions and the external world.

Paraphrase

Example (a): In *The Uses of Enchantment*, a psychological study of fairy tales, Bruno Bettelheim stresses their importance in the lives of children. They help children to understand themselves, and to make sense of the world outside themselves (53).

Explanation: The student names the source author, Bruno Bettelheim, in the lead-in to this paraphrase.

The correct in-text citation is a simple page reference in parentheses, followed by the period that ends the sentence.

Short quotation

Example (b): The author of *The Uses of Enchantment*, a psychological study of fairy tales, explains that while fairy tales "delight and instruct," they also help children "to bring some order into the inner chaos" of their minds (Bettelheim 53).

Explanation: The student correctly integrates two short quotations into the grammar of his own sentence.

The source author's name does not appear in the lead-in to quoted material. Therefore, the in-text citation gives author and page reference.

The reference list at the end of this student essay will include just one entry for Bettelheim, with necessary details for finding the original of the passage paraphrased or quoted.

Short quotation with omission

Example (c): Bettelheim explains that a child's "major problem is to bring some order into . . . his mind so that he can understand himself better" (Bettelheim, *Uses* 53).

Explanation: The student shows with an ellipsis (three spaced periods) that one or more unimportant words have been omitted from the quotation.

If more than one "Bettelheim" entry appears in the reference list, then the in-text citation uses a short-title entry to clarify the source.

Source material: *The remaining seven examples demonstrate how the student writer has drawn supporting evidence from Martin Gardner's annotated edition of* Alice in Wonderland, *and from Shakespeare's* A Midsummer Night's Dream.

Paraphrase plus short quotation

Example (d): Lewis Carroll's Mad Hatter is based on the real-life problem of hatmakers who were poisoned by the mercury used to cure felt, the material from which they made hats. A victim would develop shakiness in his eyes and limbs, confused speech and hallucinations. The phrase, "Mad as a hatter," was common in Victorian England (Gardner 90).

Explanation: The student summarizes in his own words Gardner's information. The short quotation is integrated correctly, and is used to provide necessary background for the name of the famous character.

Gardner is not mentioned in the lead-in; therefore, the in-text citation supplies his name to cue the reference list entry.

Brackets in an altered quotation

Example (e): In his note about the Mad Hatter's "famous *unanswered* riddle [emphasis added]," Martin Gardner says it was "the object of much parlor speculation in Carroll's time" (95).

Explanation: The bracketed note tells the reader that the student has changed the quotation slightly by adding emphasis with italics.

Quotation within a quotation

Example (f): Gardner adds, "His [Carroll's] own answer (given in a new preface that he wrote for the 1896 edition) is 'the Riddle, as originally invented, had no answer at all'" (95).

Explanation: The quotation, in double quotation marks, is a complete statement by Gardner, and includes information in parentheses, exactly as Gardner gives it in the source.

The student shows a quotation within the quotation, when Gardner quotes from Carroll, using single quotation marks.

Long prose quotation

Example (g): Carroll's nonsense scene continues as one of the quieter guests at the party almost wakes up:

> Here the Dormouse shook itself, and began singing in its sleep "Twinkle, twinkle, twinkle, twinkle –" and went on so long that they had to pinch it to make it stop.
>
> "Well, I'd hardly finished the first verse," said the Hatter, "when the Queen bawled out 'He's murdering the time! Off with his head!'"
>
> "How dreadfully savage!" exclaimed Alice. (Gardner 99)

Explanation: The student introduces the long quotation with a complete statement, followed by a colon.

The long quotation is set off from the essay text by indenting one inch (10 typed spaces) throughout. Note that paragraph indents are retained.

All punctuation of the original is retained. Double quotation marks are used for dialogue as in the original, and single quotation marks for the Queen's words quoted by the Mad Hatter.

The in-text citation follows the end punctuation of the set-off quotation.

Paraphrase from Shakespeare

Example (h): In Shakespeare's *A Midsummer Night's Dream*, the angry dispute between the King of Fairyland and his Queen is shown when they first appear in the woods near Athens. These powerful fairy lords insult each other in their dispute, and argue about supposed past infidelities. Shakespeare thus sets up his secondary plot, which will eventually bring the absurd clown Bottom into the lives of more important characters (II.1.60–68).

Explanation: The student uses an introductory statement and a follow-up sentence, to place the brief paraphrase in context.

The in-text citation appears before the final sentence period.

Note the special rules for references to the plays of Shakespeare. The in-text citation gives numbers as shown (II.I.60-68): act (Roman), scene and line (Arabic). The student's reference list will identify the particular edition used.

Short verse quotation

Example (i): In Shakespeare's *A Midsummer Night's Dream*, an angry meeting between the King and Queen of fairyland in the first scene of Act II begins and almost ends with Titania's command to her followers: "Fairies, skip hence: / I have forsworn his bed and company" (II.1.61–62).

Explanation: The student formally introduces the quotation with a complete statement and a colon.

The student indicates a line-break in the quoted verse with a diagonal, and one space before and after it. Capital letters and internal punctuation in the quotation are retained.

The in-text citation appears after the closing quotation marks, before the sentence period.

Long verse quotation

Example (j): In Shakespeare's *A Midsummer Night's Dream*, the angry dispute between the King of Fairyland and his Queen is shown when they first appear in the woods near Athens:

> OBERON. Ill met by moonlight, proud Titania.
> TITANIA. What, jealous Oberon? Fairies, skip hence;
>   I have forsworn his bed and company.
> OBERON. Tarry, rash wanton; am not I thy lord?
> TITANIA. Then I must be thy lady; but I know
>   When thou hast stol'n away from fairyland,
>   And in the shape of Corin, sat all day
>   Playing on pipes of corn, and versing love
>   To amorous Phillida. (II.1.60–68)

Explanation: The student introduces the long verse quotation with a complete statement, followed by a colon.

Dialogue headings are given at the set-off quotation's one-inch margin. Subsequent lines are indented an additional quarter inch (three typed spaces). Long lines are continued on the following line, indented another quarter inch.

Capital letters and internal punctuation are retained as in the source. Quotation marks are not needed (none appear in the source).

The in-text citation follows the end punctuation of the set-off quotation.

PREPARE YOUR REFERENCE LIST

The reference list appears as the last page(s) of your independent essay. Some teachers prefer the heading "Bibliography," or "List of works cited." Include entries for every source - primary and secondary - used in researching and writing your essay, even those for which you used no in-text citations.

Unless your teacher prefers a different method, use the conventions for reference list entries as explained and illustrated on the following pages. The recognized authority for essays in university English courses is the *MLA Handbook for Writers of Research Papers*. This standard university guide includes many additional variations and examples. Your high school, college or university may follow a different style guide - check with your teacher to be sure.

REFERENCE LIST CONVENTIONS

Use this summary as a guide in constructing entries for your reference list:

1. **Information:** Find the necessary information on a published work's title page or copyright page (the back of the title page).

   The following list shows the eight possible elements for a reference list entry. However, no single entry would require all eight. Elements are shown in the order they would appear:

- author's name, surname first; or title of book or article when author's name is not given
- title of article or short work in an anthology, in quotation marks
- title of book, in italics (underlined on typewriter)
- name of editor, translator, compiler
- edition used, if other than the first
- series title if relevant
- publication information: place, publisher, date
- page numbers, for article or short work in an anthology

2. **Italics:** Give titles of separately published books, and of journals, magazines, newspapers, films and television programs, in italics if your computer program has them. Underline such titles if you use a typewriter. Use quotation marks for titles of short works such as articles, short stories, essays and poems.

3. **Format:** Use the format for margins and spacing demonstrated after the next section on sample entries: double-space throughout, and use "out-dents" – first line of each entry flush with left margin, following lines indented 1 cm (one half inch) (five spaces on typewriter).

4. **Punctuation:** Carefully note details of punctuation in the examples on the next three pages. You may think that attending to every comma and period is being too picky, but a student who wants his or her work to be taken seriously must accept and follow all the conventions of literary scholarship.

5. **Arranging titles:** Arrange the works cited in your reference list alphabetically by author's last name, or by title when the author is unknown. In a title entry, ignore "A," "An" and "The" as first words.

Three typical entries from the reference list for the sample student essay on children's literature would appear as shown. Note especially the punctuation and the order of the elements in each entry.

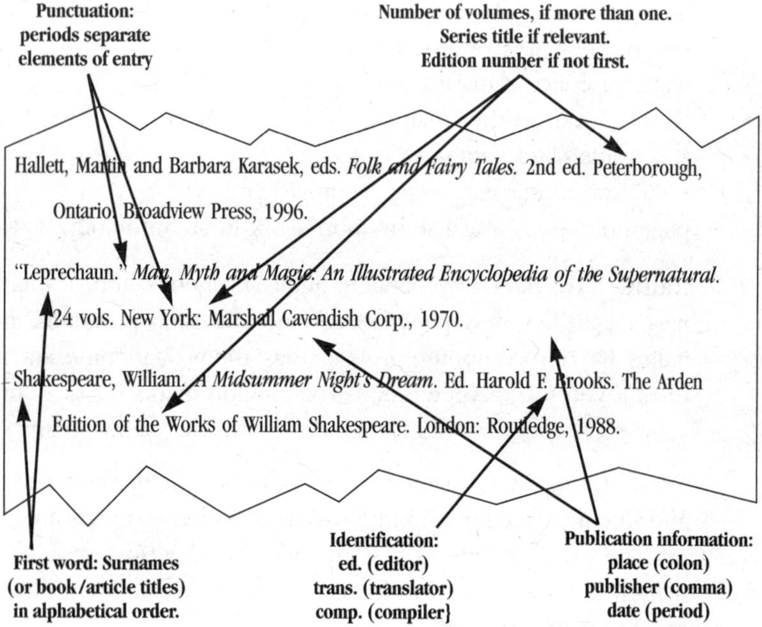

REFERENCE LIST: SAMPLE FORMS

Most types of entries for a typical senior English essay are demonstrated. Find the different kinds of sources you've used for your paper. Model your reference list entries on the ones shown here.

BOOKS	SAMPLE ENTRY
1. One author	Bettelheim, Bruno. *The Uses of Enchantment: The Meaning and Importance of Fairy Tales*. New York: Knopf, 1976. Gibaldi, Joseph. *MLA Handbook for Writers of Research Papers*. 4th ed. New York: The Modern Language Association of America, 1995. Miller, Arthur. *Death of a Salesman: Certain private conversations in two acts and a requiem*. New York: The Viking Press, 1949.
– second entry by the same author	——. *Timebends: A Life*. New York: Grove Press, 1987.
2. Anthology – one editor or compiler	Roberts, Michael, comp. *The Faber Book of Comic Verse*. London: Faber and Faber, 1942.
3. Book by two or more authors	McCrum, Robert, William Cran, Robert MacNeil. *The Story of English*. New York: Elisabeth Sifton Books - Viking, 1986.
4. Edition or translation	Shakespeare, William. *Hamlet*. Ed. Betty Bealey. The Falcon Shakespeare. Toronto: Longmans Canada, 1963. or:
– use this form when editor's notes, etc. are cited in the essay	Bealey, Betty, ed. *Hamlet*. By William Shakespeare. The Falcon Shakespeare. Toronto: Longmans Canada, 1963.
5. Book by association, institution or other corporate author	Coles Editorial Board. *Bradbury: Fahrenheit 451*. Coles Notes. Toronto: Coles Publishing Company, 1990. Time-Life Books. *The Fall of Camelot*. The Enchanted World. Alexandria, Va.: Time-Life Books, 1986.

ARTICLES, ESSAYS, SHORT LITERARY WORKS	**SAMPLE ENTRY**
6. Work in anthology *– include page reference*	Thomas, Dylan. "Fern Hill." *Collected Poems: 1934-1952*. London: J.M. Dent and Sons, 1952. 159–161. Unwin, Peter. "The Woman-Hater of Bark Rapids." *The Rock Farmers*. Dunvegan [Ontario]: Cormorant Books, 1994. 43–56.
7. Reference work *– unsigned article*	"Expressionism." *The Oxford Companion to Film*. Ed. Liz-Anne Bawden. New York: Oxford University Press, 1976.
– no publication information required for major encyclopedia	"Miller, Arthur." *The New Encyclopaedia Britannica: Micropaedia*. 15th ed. 1974. Shulman, Sandy. "Faust." *Man, Myth and Magic: An Illustrated Encyclopedia of the Supernatural*. 24 vols. New York: Marshall Cavendish, 1970.
8. Journal article *– include page reference*	Weaver, Kenneth F. "The Mystery of the Shroud." *National Geographic* 157 (1980): 730–752.
9. Magazine article *– include page reference*	Svetkey, Benjamin. "In the Wake of Titanic." *Entertainment Weekly* 6 Feb. 1998: 18–23.
10. Newspaper article *– include section and page reference*	Warner, Glen. "Minotaur Labyrinth May Be Key to City of Lost Atlanteans." *The Toronto Star* 28 Sept. 1985: H16.

OTHER SOURCES	SAMPLE ENTRY
11. Online (Internet)	Bruder, Mary Newton. "Grammar Hotline." *The Grammar Lady*. Online. Accessed 4 Mar., 1998. Available www.grammarlady.com.index.html
12. CD-ROM	Goldstein, Malcolm. "Miller, Arthur." *The New Grolier Multimedia Encyclopedia*. Release 6. CD-ROM. Grolier, Inc. 1993. New, W. H. "Literature in English: Motifs and Patterns." *The 1998 Canadian and World Encyclopedia*. CD-ROM. Toronto: McClelland and Stewart, 1997. *Shakespeare's Theater*. British Literature: The Shakespeare Collection. Zane Home Library. Dallas: Zane Publishing, 1996.
13. Television – *include title, local television station and city (if known), and broadcast date; additional information between program title and date is optional*	"*Frankenstein*: The Making of the Monster." *Great Books.* Writ. Eugenie Vink. Dir. Jonathan Ward. Learning Channel. 8 Sept. 1993. *The Skin of Our Teeth*. By Thornton Wilder. Dir. Jack O'Brien. Perf. Blair Brown, Harold Gould, Sada Thompson. American Playhouse. PBS. WGBH, Boston. 23 Jan. 1983.
14. Film / Video – *include title, distributor and date; additional information between title and date is optional*	*Much Ado about Nothing*. By William Shakespeare. Dir. Kenneth Branagh. Perf. Kenneth Branagh, Emma Thompson, Keanu Reeves. Samuel Goldwyn/ Renaissance, 1993. "Stonehenge." *Secrets of the Unknown*. Host Edward Mulhare. ABC Video Enterprises Presentation. Triumph Communications. Exec. prod. Craig Haffner. Vidcocassette. MPI Home Video, 1989.

PUT IT ALL TOGETHER: FORMAT THE WHOLE ESSAY

In preparing the final copy of your essay, follow formatting conventions from the *MLA Handbook,* as shown here, unless your teacher instructs otherwise.

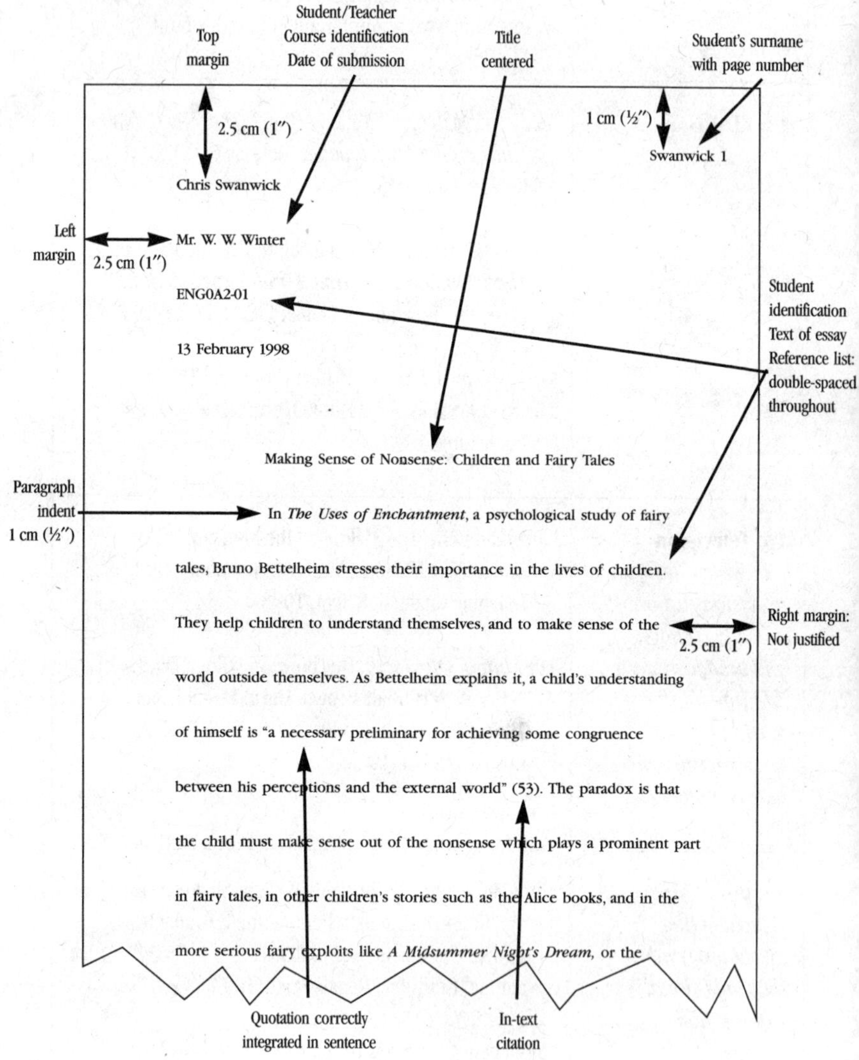

APPENDIX A

Sample independent essay with commentary

The following outline and essay represent one of the most widely used types of senior independent assignments - a comparison of two literary works. The purpose of this type of assignment is to demonstrate how different authors, in different social and historical contexts, deal with a similar important subject or theme. In our example, the common theme concerns the archetypal inner journey toward self-knowledge.

As you study the outline and the model essay, don't worry about plot or character details of the two works analyzed and compared. Recognize the pattern - the method for developing the comparison - as shown in the outline and used in the essay.

The method of development used here is called "point-counterpoint." This means that the comparison of the two works is carried out by shifting back and forth from one work to the other in consecutive paragraphs. For example, in our draft outline, Part 1 of the body shows how the writer explains and illustrates a group of related ideas first in one novel, and then shifts to the parallel ideas in the other to complete the comparison. Parts 2 and 3, covering the other subtopics, follow the same pattern. In each case, a common thread or controlling idea of the thesis statement - the inner journey - guides the writer's analysis.

This method requires skill. Look for linking words and transitional sentences that ensure coherence and maintain a logical plan that keeps the reader on track. Use these in your own essay.

Methods of development

The subtopics within an essay can be developed in several different ways, depending on the kind of essay and the purpose of the writer - to explain, to narrate, or to describe. Often more than one method is combined in the same essay.

The following three methods are particularly useful for senior English essays:

Cause and effect: Ideas, examples and incidents are organized to show a chain of events leading to an inevitable result. Useful link words and phrases: "thus," "therefore," "as a result."

Process analysis: This type of essay explains the process by which something works, often by making a comparison with something more familiar - i.e., using an analogy or extended metaphor. Useful link words and phrases: "first," "second," "finally," "similarly."

Definition: Specific terms or a larger concept may be defined in any way that is logical and appropriate to clarify the information presented. Useful link words and phrases: "This means . . . ," "that is . . . ," "therefore."

Outline: major essay on two literary works

Introduction

Broad subject: **Conrad's *Heart of Darkness* and Theroux's *The Mosquito Coast***

Limited subject: **Exploring the theme of the quest**

Thesis statement: Joseph Conrad's *Heart of Darkness* and Paul Theroux's *The Mosquito Coast* are much more than simple narratives. In exotic jungle settings, the protagonists, Conrad's Charles Marlow and Theroux's Charlie Fox, embark on spiritual quests for truth and knowledge, symbolized by a physical journey into the heart of the jungle.

Body: Part 1
Development
(2 paragraphs)

Subtopic A
with supporting
evidence:

(1) Marlow's quest
(a) Marlow's character
(b) plot summary
(c) symbolic quest / forebodings

(2) Charlie's quest
(a) Charlie's character
(b) Father's character
(c) plot summary
(d) Charlie's quest / foreshadowing about self-discovery

Body: Part 2
Development
(2 paragraphs)

Subtopic B
with supporting
evidence:

(1) Marlow's uncertainty
(a) symbolic quest
(b) reactions to others
(c) curiosity, doubts about Kurtz

(2) Charlie's insights
(a) self-discovery
(b) reactions to Father
(c) doubts, rejection of Father's idealism

Body: Part 3
Development
(2 paragraphs)

Subtopic C
with supporting
evidence:

(1) Marlow and Kurtz
(a) Marlow's changing beliefs
(b) truth: Kurtz's self-destruction
(c) Marlow's reaction

(2) Charlie and Father
(a) Charlie's changing beliefs
(b) truth: Father's self-destruction
c) Charlie's reactions

Conclusion – Reinforcement of thesis

Each of the naive and adventurous protagonists witnesses an ideological quest that has gone awry. Both Marlow and Charlie discover that a noble quest can be corrupted by passionate idealism, and this discovery has a profound but different impact on each of them. Marlow's strong sense of morality leaves him feeling alienated from his fellow Europeans, but for Charlie there is hope for mankind and society.

Major essay: sample student response

Introduction:
200 words/9 sentences

- authors and titles are cited
- limited subject is specified: exploring the theme of the quest
- method of development: compare and contrast, two novels
- subtopics are noted:
  - (1) narrators and their real journeys; ideas about symbolic quests
  - (2) symbolic quests linked to real journeys; questions and doubts, about idealists Kurtz and Allie
  - (3) ideological quests of Kurtz and Allie end tragically; different results in narrators, Marlow and Charlie

From Eden to Armageddon: The Quest in Joseph Conrad's *Heart of Darkness* and Paul Theroux's *The Mosquito Coast*

Heart of Darkness by Joseph Conrad and *The Mosquito Coast* by Paul Theroux are both compelling adventure stories, with the requisite elements of suspense, mystery, danger and escape. However, these novels are much more than simple narratives. Using exotic jungle settings, the authors explore the theme of the quest. The protagonists, Conrad's Charles Marlow and Theroux's Charlie Fox, embark on a spiritual quest for truth and knowledge, symbolized by a physical journey into the heart of the jungle. While on this journey, Marlow and Charlie witness the consequences of an ideological quest gone awry. In what is initially a noble endeavor, the characters of Mr. Kurtz in *Heart of Darkness* and Allie Fox in *The Mosquito Coast*, attempt to create an ideal society in a remote wilderness. The results, however, are tragic, for Mr. Kurtz and Allie Fox fail to recognize the personal and physical limitations of their quests until it is too late. Blinded by the passion of their idealism, both men sow the seeds of their own destruction. The discovery that a noble quest can be corrupted by passionate idealism has a profound but different impact on the spiritual journeys of both Charles Marlow and Charlie Fox.

Commentary *Introduction*

Opening: The first sentence names the two literary works and their authors, setting us up for a point-counterpoint structure of comparison in the essay. The second and third sentences state the limited subject, the "theme of the quest."

Comparison: The protagonists of the two works are named, and a brief description of their respective journeys shows their similarities. Both are on spiritual quests for truth, while engaged in real journeys into jungle settings. The comparison is then extended to explain the role of the antagonist in each story: Kurtz in *Heart of Darkness*, and Charlie's father, Allie Fox, in *The Mosquito Coast*. A strong contrast is set up within each story: the antagonist's quest goes wrong, leading to tragedy in each case. Meanwhile each narrator's quest results in enlightenment, learning from the tragic failure of their respective antagonists.

Coherence: The point-counterpoint method is already structuring this student's explanations, clearly establishing the plan we will expect to follow through the essay.

Contrast: The closing sentence of the introduction explains what the two quests have in common, but also suggests how they will differ in their impact on the two narrator/protagonists.

Body: Part 1 – Subtopic A (1)
Marlow's quest
233 words/10 sentences

- Marlow's character is sketched
- plot summary introduces the real journey: ivory trade in the Congo
- symbolic quest, and foreboding about its end, are suggested

Joseph Conrad introduces the theme of the quest at the outset of his novel, *Heart of Darkness*. Charles Marlow is an adventurous young Englishman with a strong sense of morality, duty and justice. He has a "passion for maps" and often loses himself "in all the glories of exploration" (33). He is fascinated by a "mighty big river" that resembles "an immense snake uncoiled" (33) on a map of the African Congo. Marlow is curious about the Dark Continent, and the civilized Europeans who attempt to "wean those ignorant millions from their horrid ways" (39). The "snake" eventually "charms" Marlow (33), and he accepts a position as a riverboat captain from a European ivory trading company. Marlow's journey into the heart of the African Congo is symbolic of his spiritual quest for truth and knowledge. Before embarking on his quest, however, Marlow experiences a sense of foreboding, saying, "I began to feel slightly uneasy . . . there was something ominous in the atmosphere" (36). A doctor reinforces this feeling of apprehension when he warns a naive Marlow of "the changes that take place inside [the brain] . . . of those [who go] out there" (38). Sensing the magnitude of his quest and of what he is about to discover, Marlow states, "I felt as though, instead of going to the centre of a continent, I were about to set off for the centre of the earth" (39).

Commentary *Subtopic A (1): Marlow's quest*

Opening: The first sentence states how early Conrad introduces the theme of the quest in *Heart of Darkness*.

Development: In developing this subtopic, the writer describes those qualities of Marlow's character that lead him into the quest for enlightenment, for "spiritual truth." His strong moral sense, his curiosity and his "passion" for adventure lead him into a real journey which will develop as a spiritual quest.

Coherence and unity: The use of the word "quest" at the beginning, middle and end of this paragraph establishes the link to the introduction and thesis, and keep us on track.

Supporting evidence: The writer makes frequent use of quotations from the novel to emphasize at each step of his argument the point he is making. These quotations illustrate Marlow's character, suggest the fascination he felt about his journey up-river in the Congo, and indicate the feeling of anticipation Marlow feels about the result of his quest.

Closing: The final sentence sets us up – almost in a suspenseful way – for the Marlow section of subtopic B.

Body: Part 1 –
Subtopic A (2):
Charlie's quest
357 words/17 sentences

- Charlie's character is sketched
- Father's character is introduced
- plot summary introduces real journey: family's move to Mosquito Coast
- Allie's ideological quest, and Charlie's foreshadowing of his own discovery of self, are introduced

In *The Mosquito Coast*, Paul Theroux explores the theme of the quest through the experiences of a perceptive but innocent young narrator, 13-year-old Charlie Fox. Charlie lives with his family on a Massachusetts farm where his father, Allie, a university dropout and self-taught engineer, is employed as a handyman. Allie is an opinionated man who is very critical of religion, formal education and the American way of life. Like many young boys, Charlie idolizes his father, although he resents the fact that he is forbidden to attend school, and is frightened by the dangerous tests of strength and courage his father sometimes imposes on him. He proudly states that "Father" is "the smartest man I [know]" (16), "a perfect genius" (7) who, like a god, can "work miracles" (63). Allie regards himself as an inventor, or "creator" and feels he has "the answer to most problems, if anyone [cares] to listen" (9). His employer, however, thinks that Allie is a "know-it-all who's sometimes right," which makes him "obnoxious . . . [and] . . . dangerous" (55). Allie is also a "disappointed man, . . . angry and . . . disgusted" with American society (51). He complains bitterly that the "country's gone to the dogs. No one cares, and that's the worst of it. It's the attitude of the people. . . . Selling junk, buying junk, eating junk" (47). Allie's dream is to create an ideal society in the remote wilderness of Central America, "the safest place on earth" (7). He makes arrangements to move his family to the Mosquito Coast, a bug-infested jungle in Honduras. Filled with passionate idealism, Allie sets out on his noble quest. Charlie reveres his father, and therefore does not question his views or actions. He states, "How much did I trust Father? Completely. I believed everything he said" (123). At the same time, Charlie says, "I felt like a stranger to him . . . I did not know him, he did not know me. I had to wait to discover who we were" (64). Thus Charlie embarks on his own quest – a spiritual journey seeking truth and knowledge. With a sense of anticipation and adventure, an innocent and trusting Charlie begins his voyage of discovery.

Commentary *Subtopic A (2): Charlie's quest*

Opening: The first sentence introduces the narrator of *The Mosquito Coast*, Charlie Fox. The writer briefly describes his character, as he did for Marlow, and establishes his family situation.

Development: The points about Marlow's character are here counterpointed by a description of young Charlie's character. Again, we are given a clear picture of the situation from which Charlie, accompanying his father, sets out. The major difference is that Charlie is a companion to his father's quest at first, while Marlow's quest begins in his own initiative. It is later that he finds himself following in Kurtz's footsteps. In explaining Charlie's idolizing of his father Allie, the writer misses another chance to show strong contrast between the two stories. The human object of Marlow's quest, Kurtz, remains an unknown through most of the story. His equivocal character is only gradually established, but even in the end, Marlow does not completely condemn him for the evil that has overtaken him. It is not until the end that we, like Marlow, have a full appreciation of Kurtz and how his quest has gone wrong. Theroux, on the other hand, gives us a many-layered picture (through his narrator's eyes) of Allie Fox right from the beginning of *The Mosquito Coast*. We gradually move from an appreciation of his eccentricity to a strong disgust about his character and methods by the end of the story, just as Charlie does.

Coherence and unity: Links are strong to the thesis given in the essay introduction. The phrase "theme of the quest" occurs in the opening, and the word "quest" appears twice more near the end of this section. Internal unity is helped by the references to "ideal society" and Allie's "passionate idealism." Both of these terms also provide links to the introduction, where the idealism gone wrong, in Allie Fox and Kurtz, were first mentioned.

Supporting evidence: The writer continues to support his ideas with brief quotations, integrating each correctly into the sentence where it appears, and providing proper acknowledgement of the source.

Closing: The last sentences emphasize again the real and symbolic use of a "journey" or "voyage" in the story. Again we are set up to anticipate the next developments in Charlie's spiritual quest.

Body: Parts 2 and 3

Subtopic B
Marlow's uncertainty / Charlie's insights
695 words/35 sentences

Subtopic C
Marlow and Kurtz / Charlie and Father
922 words/47 sentences

Text omitted: Subtopics B and C – Summary

Subtopics B and C follow the same point-counterpoint pattern as subtopic A. The writer explains and illustrates ideas about Marlow's quest in Heart of Darkness, *and then explains and illustrates how similar ideas are handled in the story of Charlie's quest in* The Mosquito Coast.

Conclusion:
236 words/12 sentences

- limited subject and three subtopics reviewed in first four sentences
- conclusions about the two narrators' newly acquired self-knowledge are summarized
- contrasting light-dark imagery of their quests is reinforced in closing quotations from the two novels

Totals:
2622 words/
137 sentences

Charles Marlow in *Heart of Darkness* and Charlie Fox in *The Mosquito Coast* both embark on a voyage to a remote jungle, a voyage that is symbolic of a spiritual quest for truth and knowledge. While on their journeys, the naive and adventurous protagonists witness an ideological quest that has gone awry. They discover that a noble quest can be corrupted by passionate idealism. This discovery has a profound but different impact on the protagonists. Marlow's spiritual quest reveals to him the dark heart of man, and his inherent capacity for evil. Unable to alter or escape this reality, Marlow's strong sense of morality leaves him feeling apart and alienated from his fellow Europeans. Ironically, the truth that Marlow seeks on his spiritual quest is not revealed to him in terms of light, but rather in terms of "an immense darkness" (Conrad 125). On his spiritual journey, Charlie Fox gains insight into man's need for love and acceptance, his fear of rejection and failure, and the difference between the temporal and the divine. He also discovers the limits and possibilities of the creative imagination. Unlike Marlow, however, Charlie's discoveries lead him "from darkness into light" (Theroux 362). For Charlie, there is hope for mankind and society. As he arrives back in America, Charlie says, "The world was all right, no better or worse than we had left it . . . what we saw was like splendour. It was glorious" (374).

Commentary *Subtopics B and C*

Supporting evidence: The student uses brief plot summaries to develop the complementary explanations of the two quests into the jungle darkness and into the symbolic darkness of unrestrained evil. The two narrators find their desire for understanding fulfilled in similar but unexpected ways. They both learn about mankind's capacity for evil, even in men like Kurtz and Allie who are motivated by "passionate idealism." The student prepares us for the impact the adventures have on the two narrators – new understanding about idealism, and newly acquired self-knowledge.

CUE – Coherence/Unity/Emphasis:
Throughout the body of the essay, the writer makes the most of coherence links, both to the essay's introduction and within the subtopics themselves. These links include repetition of key words from the thesis, and important words and phrases found in the two novels. The reader is constantly aware of the essay's overall plan, as outlined at the start of this commentary. Unity of subject is maintained, and effective emphasis is achieved through careful choice of supporting quotations from the two novels. In every case, acknowledgement of sources is given using correct in-text citations.

Commentary *Conclusion*

Coherence: The final paragraph of the essay neatly brings together the ideas we have seen fully explained and illustrated. A restatement of the similarities in the two narrators leads to a clear separation of them because of the different impact each experiences from newly acquired self knowledge. The writer uses the same imagery used by the two authors – Conrad's emphasis on "darkness" that Marlow discovers as part of his enlightenment, and Theroux's emphasis on Charlie's feeling of moving from darkness into a world of "splendour" and "glorious" light.

Unity: The whole essay is thus unified, using the same light and darkness imagery that the authors use. The original point-counterpoint plan has been carefully completed, bringing Marlow and Charlie together in our minds at the conclusion, to show clearly the comparison and contrast on which the essay is based.

Reference List:
176 words/10 entries

- two primary sources cited
- eight secondary sources cited – two on Conrad, six on Theroux
- sources listed alphabetically by author or title
- publication information given

Bibliography

Conrad, Joseph. *Heart of Darkness. Three Tales by Joseph Conrad.* Albert J. Guerard. Introduction. New York: Dell Publishing Co., 1960.

Edwards, Thomas E. "Paul Theroux's Yankee Crusoe." *New York Times Book Review*. 14 Feb. 1982: VII, 1.

French, William. "Theroux's Training Pays with Fiction Breakthrough." *The Globe and Mail*. 9 Mar. 1982: 15. "Heart of Darkness." *Masterplots*. Revised Edition. Ed. Frank N. Magill. Vol. 5. New Jersey: Salem Press, 1976.

"Joseph Conrad." *The Chelsea House Library of Literary Criticism, Twentieth Century British Literature*. Ed. Harold Bloom. Vol. 7. New York: Chelsea House Publishers, 1988. 3962-3967.

Leonard, John. "Books of the Times." *The New York Times*. 11 Feb. 1982: III, 31:4.

"Paul Theroux." *The Chelsea House Library of Literary Criticism, Twentieth Century American Literature*. Ed. Harold Bloom. Vol. 1. New York: Chelsea House Publishers, 1988.

"Paul Theroux." *Dictionary of Literary Biography, American Novelists Since World War II*. Eds. Jeffrey Helterman and Richard Layman. Vol. 2. Detroit: Gale Research Co., 1978.

Raban, Jonathan. "Theroux's Wonderful, Bottomless Novel." *The Chelsea House Library of Literary Criticism, Twentieth Century American Literature*. Ed. Harold Bloom. Vol. 1. New York: Chelsea House Publishers, 1988.

Theroux, Paul. *The Mosquito Coast*. New York: Avon Books, 1982.

	Commentary *Reference List*
Breadth of materials:	The list of primary and secondary sources shows that the writer of the essay has made an effort to find materials on the two authors. Aside from primary sources, these include book reviews, critical anthologies and a dictionary of literary biographies.
Depth of materials:	However, while plot summaries and large encyclopedic collections of critical materials are useful at the start of literary research, they do not go far enough. For example, for a classic writer like Joseph Conrad, a wealth of materials is available on him and his work. Many published studies might have provided the student with additional ideas about the "quest" as the central theme in *Heart of Darkness*.